GREATNESS BY DESIGN
FROM FOUNDATION TO FLIGHT

Transform Your Mindset, Build Systems,
and Lead with Purpose

Rasheeda Frazier

Published by: SheeSpeaks Publishing LLC

ISBN: 979-8-9986520-0-4 — *(Paperback)*
979-8-9986520-1-1 — *(eBook)*

First Edition

Cover Design by: Self Imaging Graphics LLC and Sha Creative Solutions LLC

Printed in the United States of America

Dedicated to every soul bold enough to walk the path of purpose,
to rise, rebuild, and reimagine their greatness
not by chance, but by choice.

To my mother,
a warrior in grace, now watching from the stars
your courage was the blueprint,
your love, the foundation beneath my every step.

And to my children,
whose laughter fuels my light,
whose belief lifts me higher
you are my reason, my rhythm, my ever-growing legacy.

Table of Contents

PREFACE

Greatness by Design wasn't born in a boardroom, brainstorm session or built in a vacuum. It came from lived experience, mine, and the hundreds of business owners and leaders I've worked with over the years.

From the very beginning, I've had a natural instinct for systems. I liked when things had structure. I paid attention to how teams moved when the processes were clear. I noticed how much easier it was to collaborate, to lead, and to grow when systems were in place. Even early in my career, I saw that disorganization didn't just cause delays, it created dysfunction. And when you're trying to lead or build something that lasts, dysfunction is expensive.

As I stepped into entrepreneurship, I saw the same issues, just louder. A lot of founders were brilliant, hardworking, and visionary. But they were operating in chaos. No systems, unclear leadership, and no support for the people around them. I recognized it because I lived it. I didn't have a roadmap either. I had to build mine from scratch.

So I created frameworks, first for myself, then for my clients. I refined them every time I hit a wall or had to pivot. I used them through wins and setbacks, through seasons of growth and times when everything felt stuck. And each time, they worked, not because they were trendy, but because they were rooted in clarity, structure, and strategy.

This book is the culmination of that process.

It's not just theory. It's not motivational fluff. It's a guide you can use, whether you're a solo founder figuring things out, a small business owner ready to grow, or a leader trying to build something sustainable. Inside, you'll find systems, tools, exercises, and real-world case studies from businesses that have applied the same frameworks.

Greatness by Design exists to help you get clear, get aligned, and grow what you've built with purpose. You don't need to burn out to build. You don't have to wing it to win. You can lead well. You can grow intentionally. You can design the business, and the life you were meant to have.

Let's get to work.

Rasheeda Frazier

INTRODUCTION
The Butterfly Metaphor

A tiny caterpillar inches its way up a branch, unaware of the magical transformation awaiting it. To the outside world, it appears simple and limited in ability. Yet within it lies an extraordinary blueprint, one that will unfold into a magnificent butterfly destined to soar through limitless skies.

This phenomenon mirrors our journey in leadership, entrepreneurship, and personal growth. Like the caterpillar, we begin life with immense potential, ambition, and a will for growth. We unleash our gift of flight through preparation, self-reflection, and transformation.

The butterfly's metamorphosis is one of nature's most magical processes. This frail creation doesn't just grow; it completely redesigns itself. First, the caterpillar consumes all it can, storing energy for the journey ahead. Then, it forms the cocoon, a place of radical change, where it breaks down at a cellular level before reconstructing itself into something entirely new. It is no longer confined to the ground but ready to take flight. This profound transformation reflects the battles we face and the opportunities we embrace in our personal and professional lives.

This book is designed to help you interweave the threads of change between personal and professional growth using the butterfly's journey as a guiding metaphor. As a business owner, you cannot separate yourself from what you do. The strength of your leadership and mindset directly shape your success, just as the systems or strategies you build in business mold you into the leader you become. Transformation is inevitable, the key is to embrace it with intention.

Our business and personal growth systems are the wings of the butterfly, unique, yet inextricably linked. One doesn't fly without the other. Strong, scalable systems give businesses wings to fly, but the owner's mindset, resilience, and leadership determine how high they can soar. This duality of leadership and entrepreneurship balances, nourishes, and elevates the operational requirements with internal development.

The following pages will walk you through the different stages of transformation:

The Caterpillar Stage: As you lay the ground, you will experience preparation, identification of opportunities, and not-so-glamorous realities. To the caterpillar, this is a period when you consume knowledge and resources to transform into a better being.

Cocoon Stage: This is a stage of deep introspection and strategic planning, where challenges are converted into opportunities for reinvention. It is when you face your limitations and reimagine possibilities to emerge stronger.

The Butterfly Stage: Now, with clarity, strength, and the wherewithal to take purposeful action, you emerge. This is a leadership and execution phase in which your potential soars as you explore your vision's limitless horizons.

This transformation does not happen in a vacuum. Much as the butterfly relies on its cocoon for protection and its wings for flight, your leadership and business must come together in a symbiotic relationship that creates sustainable success. A strong leader fuels a strong business, and a strong business, in turn, empowers the leader. The success of one feeds the other.

Transformation is not an event; it is a cycle of growth. Like the butterfly, each challenge presents an opportunity to evolve into a stronger and more capable version of yourself. A single milestone or achievement doesn't mark growth; it's a process of continuous learning and adaptation, where each new challenge refines your abilities and expands your potential.

It is not about arriving at a destination but embracing the journey, a journey defined by resilience, exploration, and constant reinvention. The lessons learned as a caterpillar, the strength gained in the cocoon, and the freedom of soaring as a butterfly all weave together to create a foundation for leading and innovating with purpose. Each stage builds upon the last, preparing you to meet life's opportunities with clarity, confidence, and impact.

This book will guide you through personal and professional metamorphosis, providing tools, insight, and strategy to help you rise and soar. As you connect who you are with what you do, you will create a balance that fosters success and fulfillment.

The G.R.E.A.T. Ecosystem™: Alignment Between You, Your Business, and Your Goals

Change doesn't just happen, it's designed. Like the butterfly, whose transformation follows a divine blueprint encoded within, your growth as a leader and builder requires structure, intention, and alignment. But unlike the butterfly, you must choose to transform. You must design the system that supports your flight.

That's where the G.R.E.A.T. Ecosystem™ comes in.

More than a framework, it's a full-spectrum model that aligns three essential elements of sustainable success:

- The structure and systems of your business
- The inner development of you as a leader
- The goals that tie your vision to action

Together, these elements form a cohesive ecosystem—your wings, your compass, and your foundation. When each part moves in harmony, you don't just build a business. You evolve as a leader. You activate a vision. You soar.

The Three Parts of the G.R.E.A.T. Ecosystem™

Throughout this book, you'll see the word "GREAT" used in different but deeply connected ways. That's intentional. "GREAT" is more than a buzzword. It's a methodology. A mindset. A movement.

Here's how it unfolds:

1. The G.R.E.A.T. Framework™ — A five-part system (Goals, Review, Evaluate, Action, Thrive) for building strong, scalable business operations.
2. The G.R.E.A.T.ness Within Framework™ — A leadership model focused on internal mastery and self-awareness. Who you are shapes how you lead.
3. G.R.E.A.T. Goals™ — My intentional alternative to traditional SMART goals. These are goals that are Grounded, Reviewed, Evolving, Actionable, and Transformative. They keep you aligned as both a leader and a builder.

Each use of "GREAT" is distinct, but together, they create what I call the G.R.E.A.T. Ecosystem™, a complete architecture for building a thriving business that reflects your purpose, values, and vision.

If it helps, you can think of it this way:
1. The G.R.E.A.T. Framework™ tells you what to build.
2. The G.R.E.A.T.ness Within Framework™ shapes how you show up to build it.
3. G.R.E.A.T. Goals™ ensure you stay aligned, focused, and evolving along the way.

The Pillars of the G.R.E.A.T. Ecosystem™: Systems, Self, and Strategic Goals

Now that you understand the G.R.E.A.T. Ecosystem™, let's explore each component in depth, starting with the operational side of building a business: the G.R.E.A.T. Framework™.

The G.R.E.A.T. Framework™: Building Strong Business Foundations

The G.R.E.A.T. Framework™ isn't just a checklist, it's a living structure that helps businesses grow intentionally in an ever-shifting marketplace. Each pillar builds upon the last to create a self-sustaining system that supports not just growth, but resilience.

G – Goals: Your Business Compass
G.R.E.A.T. begins with Goals, but not just any goals. These are what I call G.R.E.A.T. Goals™: Grounded, Reviewed, Evolving, Actionable, and Transformative.

Goals give direction. They anchor your business decisions and unify your team's focus. Without them, energy gets scattered and momentum fades.

Visualize this: A ship is sailing on the open sea without coordinates. The crew might be working hard, but without a destination, they drift with the current. Your goals are your North Star that give you direction and guide you along your journey to avoid aimless drifting.

Example: A client might set a G.R.E.A.T. Goal™ to increase customer retention by 25% in six months. This single, grounded objective drives strategic marketing, customer engagement plans, and team incentives.

R – Review: Honest Reflection for Growth
You can't improve what you don't review. Reviews are the milestones on your roadmap, so you know you're going in the right direction. They show you what is working and what is not, and where momentum is stuck, and where a pivot may be needed. A review makes you stop and ask if what you're doing now will get you what you want in the future.

Example: A quarterly review reveals your supply chain isn't keeping pace with demand. That insight prompts contract renegotiation or a shift in vendor strategy such as reassessing how you manage your inventory.

E – Evaluate: From Insight to Strategy
Review gives you data. Evaluation transforms that data into action. It's where reflection becomes refinement. You sharpen the focus. You prioritize. You decide what stays, what shifts, and what scales. It demands critical thinking, creative problem-solving, and collaboration to drive meaningful progress.

Visualize this: Evaluation is like sharpening a tool; it turns raw material into something precise and effective; strategic precision.

Example: Client feedback shows 80% of complaints center on support delays. Your evaluation leads to deploying a chatbot system and extended service hours, solving the root problem.

A – Action: Where Change Comes Alive, Execution is Everything

Plans mean nothing without execution. This is the "make it real" phase where vision becomes reality through bold, deliberate movement. This pillar focuses on converting strategies into consistent, precise actions that drive results. Action is where businesses differentiate themselves-where ideas turn into reality.

Visualize this: Think of a blueprint for a house. It is beautiful, but without builders, the house never gets built. Without action, the design never becomes a home. It just stays on the page. Action turns architecture into structure.

Example: A business launches a new premium service to improve client retention. They commit to a 30-day rollout, assign deliverables in the first week, and prepare onboarding materials and scripts. Preview calls with select clients provide feedback for quick refinements. The service rolls out through a seven-week engagement plan, with weekly reviews to track impact. By moving with intention and coordination, the business turns strategy into results, demonstrating that action, not perfection, drives growth.

T – Thrive: Sustaining Growth and Excellence

To thrive is to outlast the trend, outgrow the grind, and operate with foresight. It's not good enough to hit one milestone, you have to create a business that can sustain and adapt to future challenges. This final pillar ensures that your systems not only scale but endure.

Visualize this: Thriving is like planting a garden, not just for one season, but for years to come. It's not enough to sow the seeds; you need irrigation, care plans, and ongoing attention to ensure it flourishes. Sustained success requires systems that water your business consistently, adapt to changing conditions, and support growth long after the initial planting.

Example: You implement monthly team huddles to maintain alignment, introduce a real-time KPI dashboard to monitor performance, and launch an incentive program that rewards innovation and collaboration. These systems don't just keep the business running, they create a culture where progress is tracked, wins are celebrated, and people stay engaged. Thriving becomes the result of intentional structures that support both performance and sustainability.

Together, the five pillars of the G.R.E.A.T. Framework™ establishes the systems, structure, and strategy needed to build a business that can grow and sustain itself over time. But strategy alone isn't enough. A business can only rise as high as the leader guiding it. That's why the next framework shifts the focus inward, to the mindset, presence, and emotional intelligence required to lead with clarity and confidence.

The G.R.E.A.T.ness Within Framework™: Developing the Leader at the Center

While the G.R.E.A.T. Framework™ helps you build a strong business foundation, the G.R.E.A.T.ness Within Framework™ helps you become the kind of leader who can sustain it. This is about the internal architecture of leadership, the mindset, presence, and personal mastery required to guide a vision forward.

You are not just running a business; you're evolving into the leader that your business needs.

Each pillar of this framework begins with the same letter as G.R.E.A.T., but here, the meaning turns inward toward character, clarity, and capacity.

G – Groundwork to Success: Establishing Your Leadership Identity

The foundation of effective leadership begins with self-awareness and self-image. Groundwork is about anchoring into and exploring your values, purpose, and strengths. Those innate elements that define who you are and how you lead. Leadership is not simply a title; it is the practice of aligning your internal compass with your professional actions. Connect these elements to your aspirations. Lay the groundwork for a leadership identity rooted in authenticity and purpose.

Visualize this: A tree with deep roots can withstand even the fiercest storm. It stands tall not because of what's visible above ground, but because of the strength and stability anchored beneath the surface. Groundwork is your root system, your values, your purpose, your presence. Through self-awareness and a clear leadership identity, you create the internal foundation that allows you to grow, bend, and lead with strength no matter what comes your way.

Example: If you know your purpose is to foster collaboration, that awareness will shape how you communicate, delegate, and make decisions. You'll prioritize inclusive dialogue, create space for shared input, and lead with a mindset rooted in partnership. That clarity doesn't just guide your actions—it becomes your leadership fingerprint, influencing how others experience your presence and how your team culture takes shape.

R – Resilience and Adaptability: Leading Through Change Challenges are a given. What makes a great leader is not a way out of adversities but the confidence to face them boldly. Resilience and adaptability are the potentials that prepare leaders to embrace ambiguity, navigate uncertainty, and inspire people around them to thrive despite obstacles. This pillar focuses on emotional intelligence-building: flexibility and the ability to change setbacks into growth opportunities.

The idea of resilience means not how you stand firm but how you can bend without breaking-flexible without losing your core. This is reflected in how to hold on to core values during change. Adaptability means one can pivot strategically once the circumstances have changed and take those challenges as stepping stones toward innovation and progress.

Visualize this: It is like imagining a tree in the wind. It is deeply rooted, while its branches flow flexibly with gusts. This is resilience; a balance of strength and flexibility holding together. The tree does not snap during storms.

Example: A leader whose business is hit by a sudden downturn in the market, instead of panicking, rapidly assesses the situation, identifies the gaps, and girds his team to present new offerings. His calm demeanor and proactiveness not only keep morale high but also position the company to grab emerging opportunities. Resilient, the team remains unified, and setbacks become a catalyst for reinvention.

E – Establish Trust and Credibility: Expanding Your Influence

Leadership is a relationship. And trust is its currency. This pillar is about creating authentic connection, being transparent, and leading in a way that inspires others to follow, not because they have to, but because they want to. Leadership is not a one-way thing, per se; it is a relationship of trust, communication, and collaboration. It's about building relationships with the people you lead and creating an impact on them to be great, building an environment where everybody thrives. Expanded impact means leadership that lifts others, amplifies their strengths and empowers them to contribute to mutual success.

Trust and influence are the two bookends to leadership. To expand your impact, you need to create an environment where people are heard, valued, and supported. This happens when you actively listen, communicate transparently, and showcase the humility to learn from others. In developing those traits for yourself, you are not only leading, you are inspiring.

Visualize This: Imagine tossing a pebble into a still pond. Its ripples expand outward, touching every corner of the water. That's what a trusted leader does: his or her actions and presence create a ripple effect of trust, collaboration, and innovation.

Example: A leader who believes in transparent dialogue fosters forums for team members to share their views and ideas or give feedback comfortably. This openness develops a trustworthiness culture whereby all are at liberty to contribute. Such a team would generally become more innovative, cohesive, and focused on shared goals. Your influence expands because your team feels seen and supported.

A – Action-Oriented Leadership: Inspiring by Doing
Leadership is more than just vision, it's the embodiment of that
vision through intentional, courageous movement. People don't
follow titles; they follow presence. They follow consistency.
They follow leaders who act on what matters most. This pillar is
about execution, not as a checklist, but as a way of being.

Action-oriented leadership is less about telling and more about
showing. It's how you model commitment to shared goals, how
you carry yourself in times of uncertainty, and how your follow-
through speaks louder than your strategy slides. Your ability to
take focused, decisive action creates momentum and that
momentum becomes contagious.

True leadership demands execution with determination, clarity,
and resolve. When your words align with your actions, you earn
trust. When your actions elevate others, you build culture. This
pillar isn't just about getting things done, it's about executing in a
way that empowers people around you to rise, contribute, and
lead alongside you.

Visualize This: Think of a leader carrying a torch in a dark
forest. His light provides illumination not just for himself but
also for others to move forward with confidence. Action-
oriented leadership is that torch, the execution that steers teams
through uncertainty and shows them the possibilities when
determination meets execution.

Example: The organization's leader initiated the mentorship
program and actively and enthusiastically oversees its
development and implementation. He is deeply committed to
fostering team development and embedding a culture of
continuous learning into daily operations. This approach

encourages employees to invest in their growth, creating a ripple effect that enhances engagement and drives overall company success.

T – Thrive in Balance: Leading for the Long Haul Leadership is a marathon rather than a sprint. Without balance, even the most driven leaders can burn out, diminishing both their effectiveness and the longevity of their impact. This highlights the importance of integrating wellness into your leadership approach., enabling you to sustain your energy, focus, and influence over time.

Thriving in balance means leading with intention by setting personal well-being alongside professional goals. Your ability to inspire, innovate, and make relevant, meaningful contributions directly relates to how well you care for yourself. When you model balance, you protect your effectiveness and set an example for your team's wellness and sustainability culture.

Visualize this: Picture a conductor leading an orchestra. They guide the rhythm, ensuring each section works in harmony while allowing room for individual expression. Thriving in balance as a leader is much the same. It's about orchestrating the elements of your life and leadership to create a sustainable and harmonious flow, both for yourself and those you lead.

Example: A leader creates a quiet space for individual and group meditation sessions, allowing time for self-reflection and personal care. By participating, they demonstrate the importance of well-being and set a strong example for others to follow. As a result, they cultivate a healthier, more focused, and resilient team capable of overcoming challenges and sustaining success.

Strong leadership and solid systems form the foundation, but it's your goals that keep everything moving forward with purpose. To bring these frameworks to life, you need goals that are not only aligned with your values, but flexible enough to grow with your journey. That's where G.R.E.A.T. Goals™ come in. It is a model designed to support both who you're becoming and what you're building.

G.R.E.A.T. Goals™: Replacing SMART Goals with Purpose-Aligned Action

Most of us were taught to set SMART goals; Specific, Measurable, Achievable, Relevant, and Time-bound. While that model has its place, it was created for corporate environments that often value efficiency over transformation. SMART goals tend to focus more on checking boxes than creating real change.

But in the G.R.E.A.T. Ecosystem™, we do things differently.

You're not building a business just to meet metrics. You're not developing as a leader just to appear polished. You are becoming someone and building something that is deeply aligned, intentionally designed, and sustainably impactful. That takes more than strategy. It takes clarity, consistency, and conscious movement.

That's where G.R.E.A.T. Goals™ come in.

G.R.E.A.T. Goals™ are designed to unify the two frameworks that power this book:
- The G.R.E.A.T. Framework™, which supports the structure and sustainability of your business systems
- The G.R.E.A.T.ness Within Framework™, which strengthens your leadership from the inside out

Goals are where your inner clarity and outer action meet. Where vision becomes movement, and strategy becomes culture. Unlike traditional goals that are fixed and tactical, G.R.E.A.T. Goals™ are alive. They grow with you. They flex as your capacity changes. They guide you forward while honoring your values and the season you're in.

Let's break them down.

G – Grounded: Rooted in What Matters
Your goals must begin from within. They are not meant to impress others or tick off a list, they're meant to pull you deeper into your vision. G.R.E.A.T. Goals™ are grounded in your values, your purpose, and the unique design of your business and leadership identity.

When a goal is truly grounded, it doesn't feel forced. It aligns naturally with what you believe, how you serve, and where you're headed. It gives your energy a direction that makes sense, not just strategically, but spiritually.

Ask Yourself:
1. How does this goal reflect who I am becoming as a leader, not just what I want to achieve?
2. In what ways does this goal support or reinforce the values embedded in my business culture?
3. Am I setting this goal from alignment or from pressure, fear, or external expectation?

R – Reviewed: Revisited with Intention
In the G.R.E.A.T. Ecosystem™, growth is never static. A goal that is set once and never revisited is a missed opportunity. G.R.E.A.T. Goals™ are regularly reviewed, refined, and realigned.

This connects directly to the Review pillar in the G.R.E.A.T. Framework™, which encourages continuous business evaluation. But it also mirrors the leadership work of the G.R.E.A.T.ness Within Framework™, where you develop the self-awareness to assess if you're still in alignment with who you're becoming.

Reviewing keeps your goals current and responsive. It helps you make decisions that are not only smart, but right for *right now*.

Ask Yourself:
1. How often do I pause to reflect on my goals, and what patterns emerge when I do?
2. What checkpoints can I create to make sure this goal still fits where my business and leadership are headed?
3. When things get busy, how will I ensure this goal doesn't get buried under tasks that aren't aligned?

E – Evolving: Flexible and Adaptive
Evolving goals are not weak goals, they're wise ones. In both your systems and your personal growth, evolution is required to sustain success. That means your goals must have room to flex without losing direction.

In the G.R.E.A.T.ness Within Framework™, adaptability is essential for resilience. In the G.R.E.A.T. Framework™, evaluation leads to strategic pivots. G.R.E.A.T. Goals™ honor both. They are durable enough to last and elastic enough to grow with you.

This is how you build a future without boxing yourself into a rigid definition of success.

Ask Yourself:
1. What would it look like for this goal to grow with me, instead of limiting me?
2. Where am I resisting change in a way that may be holding back progress?
3. If I pivoted slightly, would this goal serve me and my business more fully?

A – Actionable: Clear and in Motion

A goal is only powerful when it moves. Vision without movement is a dream. But G.R.E.A.T. Goals™ translate vision into measurable, meaningful steps. They keep you from spinning in analysis or overwhelm by grounding you in focused execution.

This pillar mirrors the Action pillar of both frameworks, where movement, consistency, and follow-through create momentum. In leadership, that action builds trust. In business, it drives results. When broken into clear steps, your goals become a map instead of a mountain.

Ask Yourself:
1. What small, specific action can I take this week that moves me closer to this goal?
2. Am I avoiding movement because I want the plan to be perfect, or because I haven't clarified the next step?
3. What systems or support do I need in place to execute this goal consistently?

T – Transformative: Oriented Toward Real Change

Every goal you set should lead somewhere worth going. Not every milestone is about money or metrics, some are about mindset, impact, culture, or sustainability.

G.R.E.A.T. Goals are always aimed at transformation. They make your systems stronger, your leadership sharper, your team more engaged, or your purpose more visible. They create visible ripples in your business and invisible shifts in your confidence.

A transformative goal doesn't just get checked off. It changes something, sometimes everything.

Ask Yourself:
1. If I fully achieved this goal, how would it transform the way I lead or operate?
2. What lasting impact do I want this goal to have on my business, my team, or myself?
3. Will this goal challenge me to grow or just keep me busy?

Why G.R.E.A.T. Goals™ Work

G.R.E.A.T. Goals are the bridge between the internal alignment of the G.R.E.A.T.ness Within Framework™ and the strategic clarity of the G.R.E.A.T. Framework™. They give your growth a direction. They give your purpose a plan. And they give your leadership and business the power to evolve in harmony.

Throughout this book and in your own journey you'll come back to this model again and again. Not just to set better goals, but to ask better questions. To choose growth that fits the season you're in. To lead with intention and move with meaning.

This is how you rise on purpose. This is how you build greatness, by design.

Integration of Frameworks: Growth Through Synergy

Leadership without structure burns out. Structure without leadership breaks down.

The path to sustainable success demands both.

That's why Greatness by Design is built upon a unified, intentional system, the G.R.E.A.T. Ecosystem™ designed to align your personal growth as a leader with the operational strength of your business. In this model, your internal evolution fuels your external execution, and vice versa. It honors the truth that your personal growth and your business development are not separate pursuits, they are interdependent forces.

You are not simply running a business. You are leading a movement, building a culture, and growing into the next version of yourself with every decision you make.

To do that with clarity and purpose, you need more than one lens. You need a full-spectrum view and the structure to support it.

- The G.R.E.A.T. Framework™ equips your business with strong systems, clear strategy, and scalable infrastructure. It addresses the mechanics of how your business operates and thrives.
- The G.R.E.A.T.ness Within Framework™ develops the inner capacity of the person behind the business, you. It guides you in becoming the kind of leader who can navigate change, embody purpose, and lead with integrity and impact.
- And G.R.E.A.T. Goals™ are the bridge between the two. They transform insight into execution, ensuring your vision doesn't just stay in your head or on the page but becomes real, measurable, and aligned with who you are and where you're going.

These frameworks are not standalone tools. They are interconnected layers, working in tandem to support your evolution as a visionary and an executor. Together, they allow you to grow with balance, lead with depth, and build with precision.

Consider them the three parts of one living system: The internal foundation. The external structure. The actionable bridge. This is the G.R.E.A.T. Ecosystem™ your map, your mirror, and your method for sustainable success.

And just like any living system, transformation happens in stages, each with its own purpose, pressure, and potential. Whether you're laying a foundation, navigating deep change, or expanding your impact, the G.R.E.A.T. Ecosystem™ meets you there.

Let's walk through these stages, Caterpillar, Cocoon, and Butterfly and explore how the internal, external, and actionable parts of your journey align to carry you forward with purpose and power.

Caterpillar Stage: Preparation and Consumption

This is the beginning of your transformation, the stage of hunger, clarity-seeking, and capacity-building. Just as the caterpillar consumes voraciously to gather the energy required for metamorphosis, this phase of your leadership and business journey is about gathering the internal and external resources you'll need to grow with purpose. It's not about launching quickly; it's about laying the foundation so your next level has something real and rooted to stand on.

At this stage, the G.R.E.A.T. Framework™ helps you build the structural backbone of your business. It guides you in defining clear, value-aligned goals, assessing your operational landscape, and identifying opportunities with strategic intent. You're not simply setting up tasks, you're designing a system that will hold your growth with integrity. These early steps ensure that your business isn't just built to start, it's built to scale.

Simultaneously, the G.R.E.A.T.ness Within Framework™ calls you inward to define the leader you are becoming. This is where your leadership persona begins to take shape, not through performance, but through purpose. It invites you to ground your leadership in self-awareness, reflection, and aligned intention, helping you connect your personal identity with your professional vision. You're not just preparing to lead a business, you're establishing the internal compass that will guide how you lead it.

To bridge the inner and outer work, G.R.E.A.T. Goals™ come into play. These are not performative metrics or vanity milestones. They're purposeful, living goals that help you turn vision into action without rushing. They give shape to your momentum, clarifying what to focus on, how to move forward, and when to evolve. In this stage, your goals reflect who you're becoming and where you're headed, both as a leader and a business owner.

This is where the synergy of the G.R.E.A.T. Ecosystem™ begins to reveal itself. The operational clarity of the G.R.E.A.T. Framework™ supports your external structure. The Greatness Within Framework strengthens your internal foundation. And G.R.E.A.T. Goals™ create the rhythm and direction to help you move forward, aligned, intentional, and grounded in something far deeper than ambition.

Cocoon Stage: Introspection and Strategy

This is the hidden phase, the quiet stretch where the most profound transformation takes place. Just as a caterpillar forms a cocoon to undergo radical, unseen change, this stage of your journey is marked by introspection, recalibration, and reinvention. From the outside, it may look like you're standing still. But beneath the surface, everything is shifting. The systems you once relied on may feel outdated. The identity you once carried may no longer fit. This is the moment when clarity becomes non-negotiable, and reinvention becomes a necessity.

The G.R.E.A.T. Framework™ becomes your strategic companion during this phase. It helps you review what's working, identify operational gaps, and develop systems that are better aligned with where you're going, not just where you started. Here, strategy deepens. It's not just about building systems; it's about refining them with intention, so your business can handle more weight, more complexity, and more possibility.

At the same time, the G.R.E.A.T.ness Within Framework™ supports the personal transformation that reinvention demands. This is the internal pivot where you deepen your emotional intelligence, strengthen resilience, and learn to lead through uncertainty without losing yourself. You are evolving into the kind of leader who can navigate change not with fear, but with focus. This stage invites you to honor ambiguity, refine your presence, and anchor your adaptability so that you remain steady even as everything around you shifts.

This is also where G.R.E.A.T. Goals™ prove their power. They offer structure in the fog, giving you something to hold onto as you reorient. These goals are not fixed, they are fluid by design. They evolve as you evolve, allowing you to move with clarity even when your full vision is still unfolding. In a season where direction may feel hazy, your goals become a compass, guiding progress without pressuring perfection.

Together, the G.R.E.A.T. Framework™ and the G.R.E.A.T.ness Within Framework™ hold space for both structure and surrender. One gives you the tools to reshape your business; the other strengthens the mindset required to lead through transition. G.R.E.A.T. Goals™ stitch them together, ensuring your reinvention is not only strategic but sustainable. This is where you build your next level from the inside out.

Butterfly Stage: Leading with Impact and Sustainability

Emergence is never accidental. It is by design.

The butterfly that breaks free from the cocoon does so with strength it never needed before and with wings it never had. Likewise, at this stage of your journey, you emerge with sharpened clarity, stronger systems, and a deeper, more integrated leadership presence. You've done the work of building, reflecting, and refining. Now, you're ready to lead from alignment, not just ambition.

This is the phase where all elements of the G.R.E.A.T. Ecosystem™ come together in motion. The G.R.E.A.T. Framework™ supports your ability to operate with scale, fluidity, and intention. Your systems no longer require constant patchwork. They are designed to sustain growth, absorb complexity, and move in rhythm with your evolving goals. You are no longer guessing, you're executing with precision.

Meanwhile, the G.R.E.A.T.ness Within Framework™ reveals itself in how you lead. You carry your leadership identity with ease, not because the work is easy, but because you are aligned. Your team feels your presence. Your decisions flow from purpose. You model clarity, resilience, and balance. You're not just managing systems, you're cultivating culture.

At this stage, G.R.E.A.T. Goals™ shift from tools of traction to instruments of legacy. These goals help you refine your direction, stay focused on high-impact outcomes, and avoid the noise that often comes with success. You are no longer chasing metrics, you are shaping movements. Your goals are designed not just to drive growth, but to ensure it's sustainable, intentional, and aligned with your deeper mission.

The interplay between these three components becomes seamless. The G.R.E.A.T. Framework™ provides the strategy and structure for operational success. The G.R.E.A.T.ness Within Framework™ gives you the presence and perspective to lead from your core. G.R.E.A.T. Goals™ ensure your movement stays purposeful, measurable, and transformative.

This is where you no longer separate what you do from who you are.
This is where you lead—and thrive—by design.

Key Takeaway: Designing Your Greatness in Action

The integration of the G.R.E.A.T. Ecosystem™ forms a blueprint for intentional success. It aligns your business growth and leadership development with strategic vision and deeper purpose. No matter what stage you're in, this system will meet you there, offering structure, insight, and momentum to rise with clarity and lead with consistency.

As you continue to refine your approach, each cycle of growth will unfold with more wisdom, more impact, and more balance. This is how you lead a business that reflects your truth. This is how you become a leader who sustains greatness—by design.

The Groundwork: Building a Foundation for Aligned Growth

The Caterpillar Stage

This is where your journey begins, with structure, clarity, and alignment. You are preparing for transformation, you must feed your vision by laying down strong roots beneath your business and leadership.

Every transformation has a modest beginning, much like the journey of the caterpillar. These are times of quiet intention, laying the foundation on which greatness will be built. Though not always visible, this stage is foundational for both personal and professional growth.

The caterpillar does not rush or dream of skipping ahead to be a butterfly overnight. Instead, it focuses on the present: nourishing itself, amassing energy, and preparing for the transformation ahead. Similarly, during the Caterpillar Stage of your journey, you are called to be patient, persistent, and courageous- building your foundation slowly but surely.

Locked within this stage is a significant growth opportunity in two key ways:

Personal Awareness: You gain insight into your values, purpose, and strengths, and through self-discovery, build the core of your leadership identity.

Foundational Business Objectives: You identify crystal-clear objectives and design robust systems that create the operational skeleton upon which healthy growth can be built. As you complete this stage, your journey focuses on the preparation that underpins transformation.

Chapter 1: Setting Up for Success: Take a deep dive into self-reflection, define your purpose, and set actionable goals that will guide you through the entire process.

Chapter 2: Embracing Growth's Hard Realities: Learn to accept growing pains and the less-than-glamorous facts of creating something from scratch. Learn how to use setbacks as opportunities to pivot and use them as stepping stones toward reinvention.

Chapter 3: Your Foundation: Sync your leadership vision with systems and strategies that ensure the business is solid, sustainable, and poised to scale.

Chapter 4: Design in Motion: See how the G.R.E.A.T. Ecosystem™ comes to life through the lived experience of an entrepreneur navigating exhaustion, realignment, and sustainable growth. This chapter offers a narrative walkthrough of how aligned systems, self-leadership, and purpose-driven goals work together to create lasting transformation. Witness what happens when clarity meets action, and structure supports the leader within.

This start of your journey and transformation is not a sprint; it's about taking deliberate steps to provide the scaffolding for everything to come next. The work that you will do here, methodical, reflective, and often quiet, will set the stage for the heights to which you can aspire.

A caterpillar making its way inch by inch along the branch, knowing precisely what is next, now munching on a leaf, which provides the nutrition for a transformation as yet unimagined. Every insight you gain and every step you take in this phase nourishes your path toward becoming the leader and entrepreneur you're meant to be.

The caterpillar stage teaches us that growth is not always pretty, but it is essential. By combining personal awareness with foundational business objectives, you set a course for success and the transformative change necessary to sustain it.

CHAPTER 1

Groundwork for Success

Every transformation has a genesis, a quiet, profound whisper that speaks of potential unrealized and greatness yet to be fulfilled. But before that butterfly takes flight, it must first live as a crawling caterpillar: slow, unobtrusive, and yet determinedly set on its preparation for rebirth. For the entrepreneur and leader, the journey is the same: a foundation laid steadily, deliberately, trusting the process.

The Caterpillar Stage teaches us that the greatest transformations begin in the quiet, small moments of development. Whether slow or unexciting, your work today can shape both the leader and the business you build tomorrow.

The Caterpillar's Journey: First Steps Towards Transformation

Transformation doesn't begin with flight, it begins with focus. In the stillness of early growth, change whispers before it ever roars.

Imagine a caterpillar crawling along a sun-drenched branch. Its world is small, defined only by the leaves within reach. It doesn't rush. It doesn't waste time longing for wings it hasn't yet grown. Instead, it does what it knows how to do. It feeds itself, prepares itself, and trusts the process already written into its being. And in that quiet, deliberate rhythm, transformation is already unfolding.

Now, imagine stepping into that mindset as a leader. Your goals might feel immense. Your resources may seem hidden, your starting point too humble for the size of your vision. But like the caterpillar, your power doesn't come from how far ahead you can see, it comes from how grounded you are in what you can do today.

Every towering oak tree began as a seed. Every great leader, movement, and business started with a single decision, a single leaf within reach.

So, ask yourself: What's your next step?

Visualize This: Close your eyes. See yourself as the caterpillar, slow, focused, and unwavering. Feel the warmth of the sun on your back as you inch along the branch. Every leaf you reach for is a choice: a new habit, a new mindset, a courageous action. What's the next leaf that will nourish your journey and prepare you for the leader you're becoming?

Reflection Activity:
- Which leaves are within your reach right now?
- How can you best use today to fuel your growth?

Self-Discovery: Unearthing Your Inner Strengths

Unlike the caterpillar, whose transformation is guided by instinct, our evolution requires intention. As leaders and business owners, we must consciously discover and define who we are becoming. This process begins not with doing, but with seeing ourselves clearly, honestly, and fully.

Self-discovery is not a one-time awakening. It's a layered, ongoing return to self. It asks you to slow down and peel back the layers of identity you've outgrown, roles you've performed, expectations you've absorbed, and fears that have quietly shaped your choices. Beneath all of that lies the truth of who you are: your core strengths, your deepest values, and the intrinsic motivations that make your leadership unique.

Visualize this: Imagine a garden. The soil has been turned, and within it lie seeds to your potential, your values, your aspirations. But seeds don't grow just because they're planted. They require care, attention, and space. Self-discovery is the process of tending to that garden. You water your strengths through reflection, remove the weeds of limiting beliefs, and create conditions where your best self can take root and thrive.

When you step into leadership without self-awareness, you end up managing tasks, not guiding people. But when you know who you are, when you understand your temperament, your triggers, and your truth, you lead with clarity, compassion, and confidence. You become someone others trust not because you have all the answers, but because you are rooted in something real.

Self-discovery isn't always easy. It may reveal truths you've avoided. It may call you to make decisions you've delayed. But it will always take you closer to the kind of leader and person you're meant to be.

Lessons from the Field: Real-Life Scenario

Maria: From Doubt to Empowered Leadership

Maria had always dreamed of being a successful entrepreneur, yet when she found herself at the helm of a small team in her growing business, she felt like an imposter. Every decision she made carried the weight of her team's success, leaving her constantly questioning whether she was truly worthy of her leadership role. Was she doing enough? Was she even qualified to lead? Those questions followed her everywhere and often left her paralyzed when her team looked to her for direction.

One especially stressful day, when an important project fell apart because of miscommunication, Maria decided that something had to change. She began journaling to explore her leadership style, documenting her fears and insecurities along the way. What she learned shocked her. In the process of doing the self-awareness exercises, she learned that her strengths were not in being the most knowledgeable or authoritative voice in the room but in the ability to connect with others deeply. Maria was innately empathetic, a mentor, and a confidante in the truest sense of those words. She made people feel seen and heard.

With this clarity in mind, Maria played to her strengths. She stopped trying to exercise control and began nurturing collaboration within her team. She held one-on-one meetings with her staff to discuss their aspirations and challenges, organized brainstorming sessions where every voice was heard, and celebrated small wins to boost morale. Slowly, the dynamic began to shift. Her team became more engaged, took ownership of their tasks, and approached problems with renewed energy and creativity.

What Maria once viewed as weaknesses, her tendency to listen more than speak, empathize, and build genuine relationships, had become her greatest assets. Her team thrived under her leadership, delivering some of their best work yet. Maria learned that being a great leader isn't about having all the answers; it's about creating an environment where others can thrive and shine.

Key Takeaway: Maria's story reminds us that leadership begins with self-awareness. By understanding and embracing your unique strengths, you can unlock your potential and inspire those around you.

Practical Exercise: Your Personal SWOT Analysis
1. Strengths: What do you excel at? What is unique about you?
2. Weaknesses: What are some challenges or fears that get in your way?
3. Opportunities: What external things, perhaps a new skill, new market, or new relationship, could catapult you forward?
4. Threats: What are some things that could get in your way? And what will you do about it?

Reflection Activity:
- How can naming your strengths fuel the courage to leverage them to approach growth with a mindset of progress rather than self-doubt?
- What opportunity excites you the most and why?

Purpose: Your Compass in the Journey

Your purpose is your driving force. It propels you forward when the path ahead feels uncertain and ensures that your daily actions align with your long-term vision. Your purpose does not define what you do but gives meaning to why you do it.

Imagine you're in a dense forest and have absolutely no idea which way to go. Then, someone suddenly gives you a compass. The needle points unwaveringly toward your purpose, guiding you through uncertainty. The denser the trees and the more twists and turns on the path, the more your compass guides you to stay focused and on course.

Practical Exercise: Craft Your Purpose Statement
1. Take a moment to reflect about three moments in your life when you felt the most alive or satisfied.
2. Identify what values or principles were common to those moments. Examples may include creativity, empowerment, or connection.
3. Write a mission statement in one sentence describing your purpose.
4. Example: "To inspire others to recognize their potential and take bold, decisive steps toward realizing their dreams."

Goals: Creating a Roadmap Toward Your Vision

While your purpose gives you direction, goals are the concrete steps through which that purpose manifests. Goals structure your vision, transforming abstract aspirations into tangible, attainable milestones.

Picture this scene. You need to cross a big canyon. The goals are like the planks of the bridge. You lay them down one by one in front of you, each providing the support needed to move forward confidently. Without them, the journey feels impossible; with them, the progress unfolds steadily, step by step.

Lessons from the Field: Real-Life Scenario

Ahmed: From Vision to Actionable Goals

Ahmed had always been passionate about helping small businesses succeed. He envisioned a consulting business that would serve as a lifeline to entrepreneurs, equipping them with the tools and strategies essential for success. But as exciting as his vision was, it often felt overwhelming. It was too big, too abstract, and too unwieldy to put into action. Ahmed found himself stuck, unsure of where to begin.

One evening, sitting at his desk, surrounded by scribbled notes and half-finished plans, Ahmed realized that his problem wasn't a lack of ambition, it was a lack of focus. He needed structure, something tangible to guide his efforts and give form to his grand vision. Ahmed broke down his vision into smaller, more concrete goals, each serving as a stepping stone toward his bigger dream.

First on his agenda was hosting monthly workshops for local entrepreneurs. Such workshops on budgeting, marketing, and operations gave Ahmed an excellent opportunity to showcase his expertise and foster relationships within the business community. He also developed a clear and efficient client onboarding system, instilling confidence in new clients from day one. Each of these goals was small enough to feel achievable yet impactful enough to propel his business forward.

As Ahmed began to achieve these goals, clarity replaced chaos. His workshops gained a loyal following; word-of-mouth referrals started coming in, and his consulting business gained real traction. Breaking down his vision into actionable steps not only made his dream more achievable but also gave him the confidence to keep moving forward.

Key Takeaway: Ahmed's story demonstrates the power of turning a big vision into actionable goals. By focusing on small, specific steps, leaders can create momentum and transform their dreams into reality.

Practical Exercise: G.R.E.A.T. Goals Setting

Use the G.R.E.A.T. Goals™ framework to break your vision into aligned, sustainable action:

- Grounded: Is this goal rooted in your values, purpose, and vision?
- Reviewed: When will you revisit this goal to track progress or refine your path?
- Evolving: Can this goal grow with you if priorities or conditions shift?
- Actionable: What steps can you take today to begin moving forward?
- Transformative: What will this goal change, in your business, mindset, or leadership?

Start by envisioning where you want to be in five years. Then work backward:

- Define yearly milestones that support that long-term vision.
- Break those milestones into quarterly objectives.
- Translate those objectives into weekly tasks that build momentum over time.

Reflection Activity:

- How does accomplishing one small goal build momentum toward your big vision?

Embracing the Caterpillar Mindset

At this stage, impatience may creep in. You may long to fast-forward to the butterfly phase, but transformation cannot be rushed. The caterpillar doesn't question its progress; it trusts that each leaf consumed fuels its growth. Your task is to embrace this phase, knowing that every moment of reflection, every goal, and every small action builds the solid foundation for your future success.

Practical Exercise: Daily Growth Ritual

1. Set an intention each morning: What one action will nourish your growth today?
2. Reflect each evening: How did today's action bring you closer to your vision?

Reflection Activity:
What is the "leaf" you will consume today?

Key Takeaway: The groundwork you lay now isn't just preparation; it's the beginning of your transformation. By focusing on self-awareness, aligning with your purpose, and setting actionable goals, you are building a foundation for personal growth and business success. Growth may feel slow, but each deliberate step is a vital part of your journey.

Last chapter visualization: Close your eyes and see yourself as the caterpillar, crawling on the branch day by day toward those endless skies of possibility. What is your next step today?

CHAPTER 2

The Realities of Entrepreneurship

Entrepreneurship is often romanticized: it's a life of unbridled creativity, utter freedom, and endless possibility. Sure, all those things can be true, but the journey is riddled with times of uncertainty, sacrifice, and hard realities. Those moments often don't make it into the highlight reels, yet they are integral to your transformation. They are not obstacles to be avoided; they are stepping stones to being the leader and entrepreneur you are meant to be.

Just as the caterpillar has to wrestle to gain the strength needed for metamorphosis, so, too, must you wrestle with the weight of entrepreneurship. These struggles are not signs of defeat; they are initiations into resilience, adaptation, and growth.

The Weight of the Caterpillar: Meet the Challenges

The caterpillar inches along in growth, pushing his body towards the next stage. Movement is slow, replete with hurdles like predators, unstable weather conditions, and a tight budget. Yet he does not stop. He moves on, using each challenge as a stepping stone, knowing that unless he grows through these changes, he will never be able to soar.

This will be one of the most defining challenges you face as an entrepreneur:

- Financial Strain: Managing cash flow, securing capital, and balancing personal and professional expenses.

- Time Sacrifices: Attending family events, pursuing hobbies, or resting while juggling deadlines and securing new clients.
- Psychological Demands: Battling self-doubt, fearing failure, and carrying the weight of leadership responsibilities.

This isn't a blockade; it's a proving ground, an opportunity to build the resilience and strength essential for the next stage of your journey.

Reflection Activity:
- What have been the most significant challenges you've overcome thus far?
- How have these experiences changed your perspective and built your resolve?

Myths vs. Realities of Entrepreneurship

Entrepreneurship is often shrouded in myths that set unrealistic expectations. Narratives shaped by media, culture, and highlight reels. These myths create false expectations that can lead to burnout or self-doubt. When reality sets in many find themselves unprepared to cope. Dispelling these myths grounds, you in reality and equips you with the clarity and confidence to navigate adversity effectively.

Myths and Their Realities

Myth: Entrepreneurs work less and enjoy more freedom.

Reality: In the early stages, entrepreneurship often means longer hours, blurred work-life boundaries, and constant problem-solving. True freedom is earned after you build systems that run without you, delegate effectively, and align operations with strategy.

Myth: Success is overnight.

Reality: It's rarely about one moment. It is months, years of testing, hard work, learning, failures, persistence, and showing up when no one's clapping yet.

Myth: All you need is passion to keep the business going.

Reality: Passion is the spark, but without the catalyst of financial management, marketing, and strategic skills, the fire will eventually die down.

Myth: Entrepreneurs are born risk-takers.

Reality: Successful entrepreneurs are calculated risk-takers who weigh the possibilities of an outcome and move accordingly.

Myth: You need a revolutionary idea to succeed.

Reality: Execution trumps originality. Most thriving businesses aren't brand new ideas. They're refined, reimagined, or simply well-delivered solutions to existing problems or fulfilling a niche demand with precision and innovation.

Myth: If you build it, they will come.

Reality: A great product without distribution is a secret. You need visibility, connection, consistency, and trust. Success lies in selling well, not just building well.

Myth: You do it all yourself.

Reality: Wearing all the hats may be necessary at first, but it's not sustainable. Longevity comes from replacing yourself in repeatable tasks so you can lead with vision and strategy.

Myth: Starting a venture requires a lot of money.

Reality: Many successful businesses have started with limited capital, relying on creativity, resourcefulness, and strategic incremental growth to thrive.

Myth: It's a lonely road to entrepreneurship.

Reality: It's only lonely if you isolate yourself. Mastermind groups, mentors, collaborators, advisors, and peers are everywhere, if you're willing to seek them out and invest in connection. Go find your tribe.

Myth: When you fail, it's over; your entrepreneurial journey is over.

Reality: Failure is an essential part of the journey. Every misstep brings clarity. Every setback provides valuable lessons, strengthening your foundation for future success. Entrepreneurs who win long-term are the ones who fail forward.

Myth: Entrepreneurs are confident and fearless.

Reality: Most entrepreneurs wrestle with imposter syndrome, anxiety, and doubt. What sets them apart isn't fearlessness. It's the willingness to act in spite of fear and build confidence through experience.

Myth: Once you make money, the business runs itself.

Reality: Money solves cash flow, but not systems, leadership, or alignment. Scaling chaos is still chaos. Sustainable businesses are built on intentional design, not financial luck.

Myth: You need to quit your job to start a business.

Reality: Many successful entrepreneurs start as side-hustlers. Keeping your job while testing your model can provide financial stability and reduce the pressure that leads to bad decisions early on.

Myth: Growth always means more revenue.

Reality: Not all revenue is healthy. Real growth is strategic. It accounts for profit, capacity, operational efficiency, and quality of life. More money without infrastructure = more problems.

Reflection Activity

Reflect on the myths you once believed about entrepreneurship and how facing reality has reshaped your mindset and approach.

- Which of the myths created the most substantial expectation for you?
- How has your experience challenged it?
- How has your mindset shifted?

Lessons from the Field: Real-Life Scenario

Story 1 Robert: A Leap of Faith into Entrepreneurship

Robert had always wanted to start his own consultancy. He had been successful at his corporate job, earning a good salary and gaining a reputation as a high-caliber professional. But deep inside, he yearned to be his own boss, pursue his vision, and make a tangible, hands-on impact with the businesses he worked with. Then, with much excitement and nerves, he finally took the leap and resigned from the secure position he had held for so long to start his own consultancy.

The first couple of months had been exciting, but far tougher than Robert had anticipated. Full of ambition, he soon learned that he had underestimated what it took to be an entrepreneur. It became clear that winning new clients was far more challenging than presumed, and without a financial plan, questions about cash flow kept him awake at night. Robert struggled to balance the demands of marketing his services, delivering value to clients, and managing the day-to-day operations of his business.

Robert was determined not to let his dream slip away, so he decided to face the challenges head-on. He started attending networking events and building relationships with potential clients and partners. He also reached out to former colleagues to ask for referrals and advice. To address his cash flow issues, Robert created a detailed budget and priority list of high-impact activities that would bring in returns immediately. Most importantly, he refined his services to deliver exceptional value that kept clients coming back for more and recommending him to others.

By the end of his first year, Robert's consultancy was gaining traction. He had steadily built a growing client base, and with it came a new financial discipline that brought stability to his business. Reflecting on his journey, Robert often says that the lessons learned during that challenging first year were the founding stones of his success. They taught him resilience, adaptation, money management and most importantly, how to build strong relationships.

Key Takeaway: Robert's story highlights the unglamorous but essential aspects of entrepreneurship. Success often comes from learning through trial and error, building relationships, and staying committed to your vision, even when the road gets tough.

Story 2 Lena: From Burnout to Sustainable Growth

Lena's bakery had always been her labor of love. From small beginnings and selling homemade treats to slowly earning the status of a neighborhood favorite, things started to heat up, especially when a viral Facebook post about her bakery exploded online. Overnight, orders poured in faster than she could keep up, transforming what had once been a joy into an overwhelming source of pressure. Lena found herself working 16-hour days, sacrificing sleep, meals, and time with loved ones just to stay afloat.

At first, the adrenaline kept her going. She convinced herself that this was the price of success and pushed even harder, determined not to disappoint her customers. But as the weeks turned into months, burnout began to take its toll, leading to mistakes with burnt batches of pastries, forgotten orders, and missed opportunities to connect with her growing customer base. One day, standing in her kitchen, Lena realized she couldn't go on like this. She had poured everything into building her business, but now exhaustion was not only wearing her down, like this it was also threatening to consume the very business she had worked so hard to create.

Determined to make a change, Lena reflected on what had gone wrong. She understood that the root of her struggles lay in her inability to delegate and the absence of structured systems to support her growing business. Lena began training a team of assistants, teaching them her recipes and processes step by step. She introduced scheduling tools to manage orders and established a structured workflow that kept her bakery running efficiently, even without her constant oversight. For the first time, Lena trusted her team to share the workload, creating a balanced and sustainable operation.

With a team in place and systems running well, Lena rediscovered the joy of baking. She shifted her focus to new product development and engaging with her community. Pursuits that reignited her creativity and rekindled her passion for her business. Today, Lena's bakery is flourishing, and she often reflects on how mastering delegation and prioritizing balance not only saved her business but also reignited her sense of purpose and energy.

Key Takeaway: Lena's story demonstrates that success isn't sustainable without balance and support. By learning to delegate and implementing systems, leaders can create space for growth while protecting their well-being.

Lesson from the Caterpillar: Perseverance / Resilience

The caterpillar does not grow quickly, and neither does the entrepreneur. One must understand that challenges are an essential part of transformation. Every obstruction refines your resilience, strengthening you for the next stage of growth.

Practical Exercise: Reframe Your Challenges as Opportunities
1. List three current challenges in your business.
2. For every challenge, you will consider:
    - Lesson: What is this problem trying to teach me?

- Preparation: How is it strengthening me or my systems for what is next?
- Action: What one thing can I do today to move through with clarity?

Example:

Challenge: Overwhelmed by daily workload and unable to keep up with orders.

- Lesson: This is teaching me that growth without systems leads to burnout. I need to shift from doing everything myself to building repeatable processes.
- Preparation: I will ensure my bakery operates smoothly by training a team and creating clear workflows, even when demand spikes.
- Action: Document my key baking processes and train two assistants to help with daily operations.

Challenge: Frequent mistakes and order mix-ups. Customer service issues damaging credibility

- Lesson: This is showing me where gaps in my systems and communication are costing time and trust.
- Preparation: A reliable system will prevent costly errors, improve customer satisfaction, and free up my mental space to focus on growing my business.
- Action: Implement an online order management system and create a daily task checklist for my team to ensure consistency.

Challenge: No time for creative growth and product development.

- Lesson: Sustainable success requires balance. If I only work in the business and not on the business, I will stagnate.

- Preparation: Making time for innovation will keep my bakery competitive and reignite my passion for my craft.
- Action: I will block out two hours each week for research and development, testing new recipes, and other forms of creative exploration.

The Importance of Persistence

The caterpillar takes one step at a time, but it trusts the process. As an entrepreneur, persistence is your most valued asset. Every late night, tough decisions and setbacks are stepping stones toward your dreams. And remember, the journey is not linear, it's filled with twists, turns, and moments of exponential growth.

Reflection Activity:
- How does persistence help you to overcome past obstacles?
- What small, consistent actions can you take today to continue advancing toward your goals?

Key Takeaway: Success is not about evading the defeats; it's about embracing them as opportunities to rise and grow. The resilience you cultivate during this stage lays the foundation for the leader and entrepreneur you are becoming.

Call to Action: Making It Real

Take a minute to reflect on how far you've come.

Growth requires reflection. Take time to pause and honor the ground you've already covered. Acknowledge the struggles you've faced and how those have shaped your growth. Reflect on the lessons during the hard seasons and how it is shaping the kind of leader you're becoming.

Practical Exercise: Letter to My Future Self

Write to yourself as if one year has passed. Acknowledge the barriers you've overcome, lessons you've learned, the clarity you've gained, and the way your leadership has evolved.

Revisit this letter each year during your annual strategic planning session and see how close you have come to the leader you had described and refine as needed.

Let it be your mirror and your map.

Final Key Takeaway: The most powerful entrepreneurs are not those who avoid hardship, but those who transform it. The resilience you develop now will become the roots of the leader you are becoming and the business you are building.

CHAPTER 3

Laying the Foundation

A solid building requires a strong foundation. Just like the caterpillar consumes countless leaves to gather the energy for transformation, a business needs a strong base to launch and soar. Without firm direction, well-defined goals, and robust systems in place, even the most passionate ventures are bound to falter. This chapter will explore what it takes to create that foundation, a bedrock that ensures your vision's sustainability, clarity, and alignment.

Now imagine building a skyscraper on shifting sands. Any building without a stable foundation will collapse under its own weight. A business isn't any different. A strong foundation goes beyond the "what" of your business. It encompasses the "why" and "how" that propel it forward. This deeper understanding establishes a solid base of clarity and purpose, providing the resilience to grow and adapt over time. All of which empower you to grow without losing your footing.

Reflection Activity:
- What does "strong foundation" mean to you?
- Are your current business practices in alignment with your long-term vision?

Step 1: Define Your Vision and Goals

Your vision is the North Star guiding your business. It's the big picture that drives you forward, even when challenges arise. Goals serve as the milestones that keep you on track, guiding you steadily toward that larger vision.

Expanded Visualization: Imagine standing on a wide plain and seeing a lighthouse in the distance. The light symbolizes your vision—steady and unwavering. Your goals are the markers along your journey, ensuring you stay focused and preventing you from veering off course. Helping you avoid detours and distractions along the way.

Practical Exercise: Crafting Your Vision Statement
1. Picture your business five years from now. What does success look like?
2. Write down the difference you want to make in your clients, team, and community.
3. Now, craft these ideas into a clear, concise vision statement.

Example:
"To empower small businesses with innovative systems and strategies that ignite growth and foster sustainable success."

Apply the G.R.E.A.T. Goals™ Framework

With your vision in hand, the next step is to break it into meaningful, actionable goals. Use the G.R.E.A.T. Goals™ criteria to guide your goal setting:

- G – Grounded: Is this goal rooted in your values and vision?
- R – Reviewed: When and how will you evaluate your progress?

- E – Evolving: Can this goal shift with you if your business direction changes?
- A – Actionable: What small steps will move this forward today?
- T – Transformative: What impact will this goal create in your business or leadership?

Example G.R.E.A.T. Goal:

"Launch a new product line within six months that helps small businesses streamline their operations, with a goal of increasing monthly revenue by 20%, aligning our growth with our mission to empower through systems and strategy."

Reflection Activity:

- How do your current goals reflect your vision and values?
- Are they clear and flexible enough to inspire growth without leading to burnout?

Step 2: Assess Your Current State

Before building your foundation, you must understand where you currently stand. A structure, no matter how brilliant in design, will crumble if built on weak or shifting ground. The same applies to your business. Without a clear and honest view of your current position, your gaps, your strengths, your systems, you'll struggle to lead effectively or plan strategically. A clear assessment of your business operations, resources, and challenges provides a roadmap for improvement.

In the G.R.E.A.T. Framework™, the Review and Evaluate pillars emphasize the importance of regularly stepping back to observe what's working, what's unclear, and what's simply no longer serving your goals. This isn't about judgment, it's about clarity. When you understand the reality of your business, you can lead it with precision and vision.

Expanded Visualization: Imagine you're the architect of your business, walking the site before construction begins. You must know the condition of the land, the available tools, and the potential obstacles. You must ask yourself: What are we really working with?

Guided Business Assessment: The 4-Pillar Check-In

Use the following prompts to assess the health and alignment of your current business foundation. This isn't about having all the answers, it's about revealing where clarity and structure are needed most.

1. Vision & Purpose
   - Is your vision clearly defined and shared across your team or brand?
   - Are your goals rooted in your values, and do they reflect who you're becoming as a leader?
2. Operations & Systems
   - Do you have documented, repeatable processes for key tasks like onboarding, sales, service delivery, and communication?
   - Are you spending more time fixing problems than executing plans?
4. Financial Readiness
   - Are your cash flow, pricing strategy, and expenses aligned with your long-term goals?
   - Do you have clear financial checkpoints (weekly/monthly) to monitor performance?
5. Leadership & Capacity

- Are you working in alignment with your zone of genius—or stuck doing everything?
- Do you have accountability and decision-making structures that help you lead effectively?

Pro Tip: Use this as a quarterly review rhythm. The more consistently you assess, the faster you'll adapt and evolve.

Now that you've examined the current state of your business, identify two or three key areas that require adjustment. Choose one to prioritize, and outline a clear next step you can take within the next week.

This isn't about fixing everything at once. It's about choosing what matters most and building momentum through focused, aligned action.

Reflection Activity:
- What surprised you most about your current state?
- What small shift, if made consistently, would create the greatest positive ripple?

Step 3: Develop Systems to Scale

Systems are not just tools, they are the structural integrity of your business. Like the framework of a bridge, they support the weight of your vision and prevent collapse under pressure. They transform what works into something repeatable, turning daily chaos into predictable flow. With strong systems, you reduce decision fatigue, protect your energy, and create the conditions for your business to scale without sacrificing quality or alignment. This is how leaders shift from hustle to harmony and from short-term effort to long-term sustainability.

Core Systems That Drive Sustainable Growth

Operational Systems

Create clear workflows for client onboarding, service delivery, fulfillment, and communication. These systems should reflect your standards, reduce confusion, and ensure a consistent client experience. When your operations are organized, your business can grow without creating bottlenecks.

Financial Systems

Establish practical tools for budgeting, tracking cash flow, forecasting income, and analyzing profits. These systems help you make informed decisions, avoid financial blind spots, and maintain alignment between your financial realities and your strategic goals.

Marketing Systems

Build repeatable processes for outreach, like email campaigns, social media content, and lead tracking. Automation doesn't replace authenticity, but it ensures your brand shows up consistently, which builds trust and visibility over time.

Pro Tip: Systems aren't just about efficiency, they're about energy. When you stop reinventing the wheel each day, you free up time and mental space for vision, leadership, and creativity.

Practical Exercise: Mapping a Key Process

Choose one part of your business that currently feels chaotic or inconsistent (e.g., customer inquiries, fulfillment, lead follow-up).

1. Visualize: What does this process currently look like? Where are the breakdowns or friction points?
2. Identify: What steps are missing, unclear, or dependent on you personally?

3. Design: Create a simplified, streamlined version of this process that can be followed consistently and scaled with ease.

Document: Write out each step. Assign ownership (if applicable), and identify the tools, templates, or automations that would support execution.

Start small. Once one system is stabilized, move on to the next. Progress happens one process at a time.

Reflection Activity:
*   Which of your current systems are truly supporting your goals—and which are just keeping the wheels turning?
*   What small upgrade to one system could significantly reduce overwhelm and expand your capacity to lead?

Step 4: Align Business Operations with Your Values

Your values are more than guiding principles, they are the foundation beneath everything your business becomes. They influence how you make decisions, how you serve your clients, how you show up as a leader, and how your team operates day to day. When your values are in sync with your operations and customer experience, they create trust and integrity, qualities essential for long-term growth.

When misaligned, values become decorative words on a wall or a website. But when fully integrated, they become the framework through which your business breathes, connects, and thrives.

Think of your values as the roots of a tree. The deeper and stronger they are, the more they stabilize your business. They anchor you when things get turbulent and nourish your ability to grow with integrity, not just scale for the sake of growth. Shallow roots may look good above ground for a while, but they can't hold up under pressure. Deep roots create resilience.

This is the moment to dig deeper.

Practical Exercise: Aligning Values with Action
1. List your top three business values.
   These may include: excellence, integrity, transparency, collaboration, creativity, equity, or innovation.
2. For each value, identify three ways it currently shows up in your business.
   This could be reflected in how you deliver your service, communicate with your clients, or make decisions.
3. Now identify one opportunity to better embody each value.
   Focus on small, meaningful shifts that bring your operations or client experience into closer alignment.

Example:
- Value: Excellence
- Current Reflection: We create high-quality, detail-oriented products.
- Opportunity: Our customer service response times could better reflect our standard of excellence. We will implement a same-day response protocol to reinforce that value in action.

The goal isn't perfection, its authenticity. When your values are consistently lived out in how you operate, they create a culture your clients can feel and a leadership model your team can follow with confidence.

Reflection Activity:
- How do your leadership and management values influence your day-to-day decisions and interactions?
- Where are you modeling the alignment between what you believe and how you lead and where might you need to reconnect?
- What systems or practices could you implement to bring your values from abstract principle into daily practice?

Step 5: Build Accountability into Your Foundation

Accountability isn't just about checking boxes or hitting deadlines, it's the ongoing practice of staying rooted in your intentions and showing up for what you've committed to, even when no one is watching. It's how you bridge the gap between who you are now and the leader you're becoming.

In a business built by design, accountability is woven into the everyday, not tacked on when things go wrong. It serves as a quiet contract between you and your purpose. When done right, it's not pressure, it's clarity.

Fresh Accountability Strategies to Anchor Your Growth
- Voice Notes to Future You
  Once a week, record a short voice memo reflecting on your decisions, lessons, and progress. Listen back at the end of each month to track your evolution. It's a powerful way to hear your own growth in real time and reconnect with your 'why' on the days it feels far away.
- Walk It Out Reflections
  Choose one day a week to reflect while walking. Leave your phone behind and give yourself a guiding question like, "Where did I show up with intention this week?"

Movement fuels insight, and this practice reconnects your body and leadership instincts.

- Schedule Check-Ins
  Accountability thrives in relationships. Schedule regular check-ins with a mentor, advisor, peer, or trusted team member to recalibrate and reflect. These conversations keep your goals visible and your thinking sharp.
- Celebrate Milestones Not Just Outcomes
  Progress deserves to be acknowledged, not just the big wins. Celebrate when you follow through, stay consistent, or pivot with clarity. Recognition builds momentum and keeps your journey energized.

Pro Tip: Accountability doesn't require pressure. It requires presence.

Reflection Activity:
- How are you currently anchoring yourself to your goals and values on a weekly basis?
- Which of these strategies could help you stay committed without overloading your schedule?
- How might you design your own accountability rhythm, one that reflects how you work best?

Lessons from the Field: Real-Life Scenario

Story 1: Sarah's Artisan Shop

Sarah's artisan jewelry store was born from a passion project, a creative outlet where she designed unique pieces, each one cherished by the customers. Her designs were intricate and personalized and told a very detailed story. As word of her talent spread, demand increased, and soon enough, Sarah found herself juggling orders from customers across the region. This was a great success, but it also exposed a glaring problem in her business: her production process was neither consistent nor organized.

With a sudden increase in orders, Sarah found herself struggling to cope. Some tasks took longer than anticipated, while others were rushed, and Sarah was dissatisfied with their quality. Without an inventory system in place, she often ran out of essential materials, forcing her to make urgent trips to suppliers. Customers began to complain about delays, and Sarah felt that she was losing control over her burgeoning business.

Determined to get to the bottom of the problem, Sarah dedicated a weekend to mapping out her entire production process, analyzing each step carefully. She identified the bottlenecks: the lack of preparation for running out of materials and failure to prioritize custom orders. She implemented an inventory management system to track her supplies and set up automatic restocking alerts to address this. She also created a production schedule, breaking down the tasks into manageable steps, allowing her to prioritize orders based on deadlines and complexity more efficiently.

The changes were transformational. Having implemented new systems, Sarah eliminated production delays, and ensured every piece was delivered on time, and met her high standards. With confidence in her streamlined operations, she took on more oversized orders, knowing her business could meet the demand efficiently.

The newfound organization freed up her time, allowing her to focus on design innovation and fostering strong customer relationships. As her artisan shop grew into a thriving business,

Sarah often reflected on how addressing inefficiencies not only supported her creativity and passion but also enhanced the customer experience and gave her the space to think strategically about the future of her brand.

Key Takeaway: Sarah's story perfectly shows how strong systems create stability, allowing the business to grow without overwhelming the owner. Leaders can build a foundation for growth and success by identifying inefficiencies and implementing solutions.

Story 2: Theo: Defining His Niche to Build Success

Theo has always been good at problem-solving and has a passion for growing businesses. He offered a range of solutions, from operations and marketing to financial strategy, hoping to get as many clients as possible. His approach worked well in the beginning with several small projects across various industries. However, he started to get overwhelmed with his business growth. His services weren't focused, and his marketing was piecemeal; therefore, many of his prospective clients didn't know what exactly he specialized in.

One day, Theo decided to take a step back and assess the health of his business. He reviewed his projects over the past year, analyzing which ones had been most fulfilling and profitable. A clear pattern emerged: his work with mid-sized technology firms had had the most impact. These clients appreciated his expertise in smoothing out their operations and scaling their businesses, while Theo found their innovative environments invigorating.

Armed with this insight, Theo took the bold step of rebranding to provide niche services. He refocused and zeroed in entirely on consulting for mid-sized technology companies, calibrating his solutions to address their unique challenges. Theo revised his marketing strategy to create messaging that spoke directly to this audience, highlighting his proven results in the tech sector. To build relationships and establish his name as an expert within the industry, he attended tech conferences and networking events.

The results were amazing. In a year, Theo had doubled his income and attracted high-value clients willing to work with a person who truly understood their special needs. The deeper relations with his clients improved not only the outcomes of his projects but also created a steady stream of referrals.

Reflecting on this journey, Theo often says that narrowing his focus was a watershed in his business. He developed a sustainable model by matching his offerings to his strengths and passions, enabling him to render extraordinary value to his clients and to position himself as the first among equals in his field.

Key Takeaway: Theo's story demonstrates the power of focus in building a thriving business. By identifying and committing to a niche, leaders can align their services with their strengths and create deeper, more impactful relationships with their clients.

Reflection Activity:
- What lessons from these stories can I apply to my business?

At this point, the caterpillar eats all of the fuel it will need to become a butterfly. Likewise, the time and energy you invest in laying a solid foundation will be the fuel that propels your business forward. A clear vision, well-structured systems, and strong alignment with your values provide the foundation for your business to not only survive but truly thrive.

Call to Action: Strengthen Your Foundation

- Take another look at your vision statement and your SMART goals.
- Identify one key system you could streamline this week.
- Now, consider how your values are or aren't showing up in your business. Commit to making one change.

This call to action is a repetitive process and should be done until your business systems are strong enough to support the direction and growth of your business.

Ground Laid, Vision Set

Sarah and Theo's stories remind us that foundational work is not glamorous, but it is transformational. Whether it's clarifying your niche, realigning your systems, or reconnecting to your purpose, these moments of grounding are what give your business the strength to scale and give you the capacity to lead.

By now, you've done the deep work of setting your business foundation. You've clarified your vision, assessed your gaps, designed meaningful systems, reconnected to your values, and created space for accountability that supports your leadership, not just your output.

Now it's time to step into the next phase.

Just like the caterpillar enters the cocoon to undergo internal transformation, you, too, are ready to shift inward. You've grounded your vision and set the structure. Now it's time to enter the next phase, where what's unseen begins to transform everything you've built.

In the next part of the book, we'll explore the mindset, emotional resilience, and personal evolution required to rise into the leader your business needs next.

Before we move into the deeper layers of leadership in Part 2, let's look at what the full G.R.E.A.T. Ecosystem™ looks like in real life, when structure, self, and purpose come into alignment.

CHAPTER 4

Design in Motion: Walking Through the G.R.E.A.T. Ecosystem™ in Real Life

When Structure Meets Soul

Transformation isn't just about doing more, it's about aligning everything you're doing with who you are becoming. The G.R.E.A.T. Ecosystem™ is your architecture for that alignment. It brings together three pillars: the business foundation, the leader within, and the purpose-aligned goals that hold it all together. When activated, it becomes the difference between chasing success and building greatness.

Let me introduce you to Jasmine, a gifted, heart-centered entrepreneur whose story illustrates what happens when all three pillars of the ecosystem come alive.

Jasmine's Starting Point: The Edge of Burnout

Jasmine was three years into her business, a handcrafted wellness brand rooted in holistic healing for women of color. Her products were beautiful, her following was loyal, and her passion was undeniable. But behind the scenes, she was unraveling.

She was fulfilling orders until 2 AM, answering DMs at stoplights, and holding her breath every month to see if she could cover inventory and rent. There were moments of brilliance, viral posts, sellout markets, glowing testimonials, but nothing sustained. She felt like she was holding something powerful with no container to hold it in.

In her words:
"I built a brand to heal others, but I'm the one who's breaking."

That's when she found her way to the G.R.E.A.T. Ecosystem™.

Part 1: The G.R.E.A.T. Framework™ — Building Strong Business Foundations

Jasmine had passion. What she needed now was structure. We started with the first pillar of the ecosystem, her business operations and used the G.R.E.A.T. Framework™ to rebuild the foundation from the inside out.

G – Goals: Your Business Compass
We clarified her true business direction. Instead of "sell more" or "grow bigger," her compass became:

- To create accessible wellness rooted in culture and ritual.
- To build a subscription model that stabilized income.
- To create a business model that didn't require burnout to succeed.

She stopped chasing trends and started designing with focus.
R – Review: Honest Reflection for Growth

Together, we audited her business:
- 25+ SKUs but only 5 consistently profitable
- No pricing structure rooted in margin
- No order fulfillment system
- No clear boundaries around time

This wasn't to shame her. It was to see clearly the foundation for any redesign.

E – Evaluate: From Insight to Strategy

From the audit, we created a strategic shift:

- Eliminated 40% of products to highlight her core ritual line
- Adjusted prices to reflect true costs and value
- Mapped a workflow for batching production and customer service
- Created a team onboarding doc to prepare for future hiring

Her business began to feel intentional for the first time.

A – Action: Where Change Comes Alive

We didn't just make plans. We moved:

- Launched her first 3-month ritual subscription box
- Rebuilt her Shopify backend for clarity and conversion
- Rewrote her brand story to center her healing philosophy
- Added a CRM system to nurture repeat customers

Within 60 days, she was generating consistent weekly revenue without chasing every dollar.

T – Thrive: Sustaining Growth and Excellence

We created monthly systems to protect her progress:

- CEO Time: 2 hours every Friday for review + planning
- Subscription metrics tracked with a simple dashboard
- Quarterly audits for inventory, pricing, and customer satisfaction
- Scheduled digital detox weekends every quarter

The chaos lifted. Her business became a space she could breathe in again.

Part 2: The G.R.E.A.T.ness Within Framework™ — Developing the Leader at the Center

With structure in place, Jasmine faced the deeper challenge, her own voice, fears, and mindset. This is where the G.R.E.A.T.ness Within Framework™ came in: building the leader capable of stewarding sustainable success.

G – Groundwork to Success: Establishing Your Leadership Identity
Jasmine had never called herself a leader. She was "just trying to get it all done." We redefined her role not as a doer, but a designer and guide. She wrote a leadership identity statement:

I am a creative founder, a culture-shifter, and a visionary builder. I lead with care and clarity.

It became her daily grounding ritual.

R – Resilience and Adaptability: Leading Through Change
Scaling required delegation and discomfort. When her first packaging vendor dropped the ball, she didn't spiral. She paused, pivoted, and communicated. She learned to adapt without abandoning herself.

She also began celebrating bounce-backs not just wins.

E – Establish Trust and Credibility: Expanding Your Influence
Jasmine had held back from thought leadership. With renewed confidence, she began writing monthly wellness reflections, appearing on a niche podcast, and mentoring another maker behind the scenes.

Her influence wasn't about ego, it was about sharing the energy of her ecosystem.

A – Action-Oriented Leadership: Inspiring by Doing
She didn't just delegate tasks. She modeled presence, empathy, and boundaries for her new assistant. She made decisions faster. She said no without apology. Her team followed her example because she embodied it.

T – Thrive in Balance: Leading for the Long Haul
No more 2 AM fulfillment. Jasmine worked 4 days/week. She took two weeks off midyear. She meditated before launches and reviewed analytics with joy. Her business became a tool for well-being not a barrier to it.

Part 3: G.R.E.A.T. Goals™ — Replacing SMART Goals with Purpose-Aligned Action

With systems and self now in alignment, Jasmine set G.R.E.A.T. Goals™ not performance metrics, but deeply intentional, soul-aligned action steps.

G – Grounded: Rooted in What Matters
Her goals were centered on her mission:
- Support women of color in daily healing practices
- Create intergenerational wellness conversations
- Build income to support community-based giving

R – Reviewed: Revisited with Intention
Each month, she reviewed goals through reflection, not guilt. What worked? What felt aligned? What didn't? She released goals that no longer fit and added new ones with clarity.

E – Evolving: Flexible and Adaptive
When her second quarter launch underperformed, she didn't panic. She adjusted messaging, added storytelling, and gave herself grace. She evolved in real time.

A – Actionable: Clear and in Motion
Her goals weren't vague. They were living:

- Launch Summer Ritual Box by July 15
- Reach 150 subscribers by September
- Schedule 2 community conversations on IG Live per quarter

T – Transformative: Oriented Toward Real Change
These weren't tasks. They were mirrors. They changed how she thought, how she led, and how she lived. She became more spacious, more certain, more sovereign.
What Jasmine Gained

Within six months, Jasmine had:

- Doubled her monthly revenue through aligned offerings
- Reduced her work hours by 30%
- Built a team of 2 part-time contractors
- Grown her email list and customer retention
- Felt more powerful in her skin than she had since the day she launched

But the real win?

"I'm finally running a business that feels like it belongs to me. Not the market. Not the hustle. Me."
Your Turn: What Will You Design?

The G.R.E.A.T. Ecosystem™ isn't something you memorize. It's something you live.

- Where is your business asking for structure?
- Where is your leadership asking for healing?
- What would it mean to set goals that nourish *you* as much as they grow your results?

You don't have to force a breakthrough.
You just have to design one.

PART 2

The Inner Shift: Strategy, Stillness, and Self-Alignment

The Cocoon Stage

Now that your foundation is in place, it's time to go inward. This stage is where transformation deepens, through reflection, recalibration, and strategic realignment. This is where you reimagine what's next.

The cocoon is a place of radical transformation whereby the caterpillar sheds its old form and prepares for its next step. From the outside, it may appear to be a place of no movement, even stagnation. Yet, from the inside, a miracle is taking place. To the entrepreneur and leader, this stage signifies the period of introspection and strategy building needed to translate vision into action.

The Cocoon Stage beckons you to turn inward while refining your outward strategies for the journey ahead. Pause, evaluate, and strengthen the systems, habits, and beliefs that have carried you to this point. Some will need strengthening, and others need shedding. It's not just about planning for growth; it's about growing into the kind of leader who can sustain and lead such growth.

The Duality of the Cocoon Stage

The Cocoon Stage encompasses two key areas of growth:

Introspection: Turn inward as a leader. Examine your emotional resilience, reassess your purpose, and ensure your goals align with your vision.

Business Strategic Planning: Identify strengths and weaknesses, refine your systems, and develop actionable strategies for enduring success.

Visualize this: Inside the caterpillar's cocoon, its body is dissolving. It sheds old structures that are no longer serving it.

Yet within this process, something amazing is taking shape: wings are forming, strength is building, and soon, it will emerge ready to fly. Likewise, this is your time to break down ineffective habits, systems, and mindsets that no longer serve your vision and rebuild with purpose, preparing for your next stage of success.

A Time of Reflection and Strategy

This phase requires much-needed doses of patience and courage. It can be uncomfortable to reflect on, as it requires facing areas where growth is needed. Strategy requires clarity and focus, ensuring that your plans align with your personal and professional goals. The cocoon teaches us that transformation is not a quick fix but a deliberate preparation for an intentional shift to set the stage for lasting success.

Reflection Activity:
- Identify the specific beliefs, habits, or systems holding you back from your next growth phase.
- What strengths can you develop to position you for a strong future now?

What You Will Discover in the Following Chapters

The Cocoon Stage is where strategy meets introspection.

Chapter 5: Resilience and Adaptability - Developing emotional intelligence and agility to lead through change.

Chapter 6: Strategic Realignment - Reevaluating and refining your goals, systems, and strategies to align with and support your vision.

Chapter 7: Elevate Your Influence - Increasing your leadership presence to inspire trust, collaboration, and action.

Key Takeaway: The Cocoon Stage is where transformation becomes intentional. Through a balance of introspection and strategic planning, not only do you prepare your business for its next stage of growth, but you also evolve into the leader who can sustain it. This phase reinforces that actual growth demands reflection, strategy, and the willingness to release what no longer aligns with your vision.

Call to Action: Now, as you enter the Cocoon Stage, take a moment to reflect on your journey so far. What habits, systems, or mindsets must evolve to support your growth? What strengths have you developed that will help you navigate this next phase of transformation?

CHAPTER 5

Resilience and Adaptability: Thriving Through Change

Transformation is rarely a seamless process. It is messy, unpredictable, and often uncomfortable. Inside the cocoon, the caterpillar doesn't just rest; it dissolves completely before emerging as something new. Similarly, as a leader or entrepreneur, this level of transformation requires embracing discomfort, uncertainty, and change and developing the resilience and adaptability that will foster thriving in the face of the unexpected.

This chapter will walk you through facing your most difficult moments with intention. It's not about avoiding change but mastering it. It's about building the tools that will reshape you and your business for the next phase of growth.

The Cocoon Stage: A Time of Transformation

Imagine the caterpillar in its cocoon. To the outside world, it may seem like a statue, still, stagnant, even. But inside, a transformation is taking place: cells realign, wings start to form, and an entirely new being begins to take shape. For you, the cocoon stage represents those moments of reflection and struggle where you meet your challenges head-on and reshape who you are and how you lead.

Reflection Activity:

- Think of a time when you faced a significant challenge in your business or personal life.
- What internal shift happened inside of you as a result?

What Resilience Looks Like in Leadership

Resilience is not about avoiding struggle; it's about thriving within it. Resilient leaders don't view challenges as obstacles; they recognize them as opportunities and stepping stones for growth, and they use each failure as fuel for their transformation and progress.

Lessons from the Field: Real-Life Scenario

Carlos: Adapting to Supply Chain Struggles

Carlos had put a lot of effort into building his online store, specializing in handmade home décor. He had been fastidious about the smallest details, and his commitment to quality had attracted a loyal base of customers. All that changed, however, when delays in the supply chain started to percolate throughout his operations. The raw materials he relied on for his products were stuck in transit, and delivery timelines stretched weeks beyond what his customers had been promised. Emails of frustration and complaints began flooding in, and Carlos felt the weight of it all pressing down on him. Sales dropped, and he began questioning whether his business could survive.

At first, Carlos was paralyzed by the magnitude of the problem. The delays were totally beyond his control, and the uncertainty left him feeling powerless. However, when he took a step back, he came to understand that he still had control over one crucial factor: how he responded to the situation. Instead of retreating, he chose to tackle the challenge head-on.

Carlos began by being transparent with his customers. He sent personalized emails explaining the delays and sincerely apologized for the inconvenience caused. He also offered discounts on pre-orders as a token of appreciation for their patience. Additionally, he provided free shipping for affected orders. His proactive approach helped ease frustrations and reassured his customers that he was doing everything possible to resolve the problem.

Next, Carlos took steps to stabilize his supply chain. He researched local suppliers to secure the needed materials, even at a slightly higher cost. Sourcing locally reduced production time and granted him some control over his inventory levels. What began as a short-term fix evolved into a long-term advantage, strengthening his relationships with local partners.

Within a few months, Carlos successfully stabilized his business. Many customers who had initially expressed frustration became his strongest advocates, praising his transparency and dedication. By focusing on what he could control and taking decisive action, Carlos saved his business and built a stronger, more resilient foundation for the future.

Key Takeaway: Carlos's story powerfully illustrates the impact of resilience and adaptability in leadership. When faced with challenges beyond control, shifting focus to solutions rather than dwelling on the problem and maintaining open communication can transform a crisis into building trust and loyalty.

Characteristics of Resilient Leaders:
- They view challenges as learning opportunities.

- They maintain composure under pressure.
- They focus on solutions, not problems.

Reflection Activity:
- How do you usually react to setbacks?
- What are some things you can do to reframe challenges into opportunities?

Building Emotional Intelligence for Adaptability

Emotional intelligence, which is self-awareness of one's feelings and empathy for others, is at the core of resilience. It empowers leaders to navigate challenges with clarity and compassion, even in turbulent times.

Practical Exercise: Emotional Check-In
1. At the end of each day, take a moment to reflect on the following questions:
   - What emotions did I feel most strongly today?
   - How did these emotions impact my decisions and interactions?
2. Think of one moment where you could have responded differently. Write down how you will approach a similar situation in the future.

Reflection Activity:
- How does being aware of your emotions help you to more effectively meet challenges in your life?

Resilience: Turbulence
Turbulence is inevitable in business and leadership. There are always unexpected changes, setbacks, or emotional disruptions. Resilience is what allows you to stay grounded and keep moving through those moments. But it's not about brute force or

pushing through at all costs. Resilience is the inner strength to adapt under pressure. That's where adaptability comes in, the ability to pivot, shift perspectives, and reorganize in response to change. Like the caterpillar in the cocoon, you must learn to let go of old ways and reorganize your mindset and systems for what's next.

Lessons from the Field: Real-Life Scenario

Priya: Reinventing Her Café Through Adaptability

Priya had poured her heart and soul into building her café from the ground up. It was cozy with a homely environment where regulars came to relax, enjoy a cup of coffee, and savor her famous homemade cakes. Business had always been steady, with customers coming in through the day, creating a warm and welcoming buzz. But then everything changed one day when a big construction project started nearby. Foot traffic dwindled to almost nothing, and Priya's once bustling cafe now sat eerily empty for hours on end. Her daily sales began to plummet, and the sense of community she had worked so hard to cultivate appeared to disappear almost overnight.

At first, Priya was overwhelmed by the sudden change. She couldn't control the construction or force the customers to wade through chaos just to come to her place. For a couple of weeks, she had decided to scale back operations or even temporarily close her doors. But rather than give up in the face of the challenge, Priya decided to adapt. Since her customers could not make it to her, she would bring the café to them.

Priya quickly pivoted to delivery services and developed an online ordering system. She partnered with local drivers to deliver her coffee and baked products to customers' homes and offices. She also revamped her social media by sharing behind-the-scenes glimpses of her kitchen and promoting her new delivery options. To sweeten the deal, she introduced exclusive online promotions like discounts on bulk orders and free delivery for loyal customers.

The results were transformative. Customers who once came to her for an experiential treat now adopted the convenience of having her treats delivered to their doorsteps. Her online platform enabled her to extend her reach beyond the neighborhood, attracting new customers who had never entered her café. In just a few months, Priya's sales returned to pre-construction levels and began to surpass them.

Looking back, Priya realized the ability to pivot hadn't just saved her business; it had expanded it in ways she hadn't imagined. Along the way, she opened new revenue streams and built a brand reputation for being adaptable and innovative, meeting her customers where they were.

Key Takeaway: Priya's story demonstrates that adaptability is a superpower for leaders. By embracing change and seeking creative solutions, you can transform challenges into opportunities to grow and thrive.

Tips for Developing Adaptability

1. Cultivate a Growth Mindset: See failures as learning opportunities.
2. Be Curious: Continuously explore new tools, strategies, and perspectives.
3. Practice Flexibility: Be willing to adjust your approach when things aren't working.

Reflection Activity:

- Where in your business or leadership approach can you become more flexible?
- What new options might open up by shifting your perspective?

The Power of the 5 Whys in the Cocoon Stage

The 5 Whys technique is a powerful tool for uncovering the root causes of challenges. By repeatedly asking "Why?" you peel back layers of the problem to get closer to its core.

Example: High Employee Turnover

1. Why? Employees feel overworked.
2. Why? Tasks are not evenly distributed.
3. Why? We don't have a clear system for delegating responsibilities.
4. Why? Leaders haven't prioritized delegation.
5. Why? Strategic planning time hasn't been set aside.

Root Cause: Poor task delegation is caused by insufficient time for strategic planning.

Action Plan:

- Invest time in developing a task allocation system.
- Empowering your team leaders to implement and monitor the system.

Reflection Activity:

- Choose one recurring problem in your business.
- Use the 5 Whys method to uncover its root cause.
- Develop an action plan to address it.

Lessons from the Cocoon: Growth Through Challenge

The cocoon is not a comfort zone. It is where the disassembling and reassembling happen, a time when you confront the parts of your life and business that must change. Discomfort is not the enemy; it is a harbinger of transformation.

Practical Exercise:
1. Write down three challenges that you are dealing with right now.
2. For each one, ask yourself:
   - Lesson Learned: What is this challenge teaching me?
   - Growth: How will overcoming it prepare me for future success?
   - Action: What is one step I can take today to address it?

Example 1 – Business Systems Challenge
- Challenge: My marketing efforts aren't yielding results.
- Lesson Learned: I need to better understand my audience's actual needs instead of assuming I know what they want.
- Growth: Learning how to listen more deeply and adapt my approach will make me a more responsive and effective leader in every area of my business.
- Action: Draft and send a short customer survey this week to gather feedback, then schedule time to analyze the responses and refine my messaging.

Example 2 – Team/Collaboration Challenge
- Challenge: I avoid giving constructive feedback to my team because I don't want to be perceived as harsh.

- Lesson Learned: Avoiding difficult conversations creates more confusion and blocks growth for them and for me.
- Growth: Practicing honest, compassionate communication will help me become a stronger, more respected leader and create a healthier team culture.
- Action: Schedule one-on-one check-ins with each team member to review goals and offer clear, supportive feedback.

Example 3 – Personal/Mindset Challenge
- Challenge: I often doubt myself before making important decisions, which causes delays and second-guessing.
- Lesson Learned: I've been outsourcing my confidence to external validation instead of building trust in my own instincts.
- Growth: Strengthening my self-trust will help me make faster, more aligned decisions and lead from a place of clarity.
- Action: Create a personal decision-making ritual. Journal through options, review my values, and commit within 48 hours.

The Caterpillar's Secret: Patience and Persistence

Transformation takes time. Just like the caterpillar spends weeks in its cocoon, your transformation as a leader and entrepreneur demands patience and persistence. Each challenge you face will build up the resilience and adaptability needed for your next phase.

Reflection Activity:
- How can you cultivate patience and persistence through your present challenges?

- What small, consistent actions can you take to keep moving forward?

Key Takeaway: Resilience and adaptability are not innate traits; they are skills honed through practice and self-awareness. Each challenge you encounter is an opportunity to strengthen these skills to prepare for your journey.

Call to Action: Build Your Resilience
1. Reflect on a recent challenge and what it taught you.
2. Commit to one new habit, like a daily emotional check-in, to strengthen your resilience.
3. Embrace the discomfort of growth, knowing you are being fashioned into the leader you are meant to be.

Resilience, at its core, is adaptive. It's not just the ability to survive difficulty it's the wisdom to grow through it and emerge with greater clarity. But as you evolve, your systems, strategies, and structures must evolve too. Misalignment is often not a failure of effort, but a signal that you've outgrown what once worked. The next phase of your journey invites you to pause with purpose, to reflect, recalibrate, and realign every part of your business and leadership with the version of you that's emerging. Because thriving through change isn't just personal, it's strategic. Let's step deeper into the cocoon and design from the inside out.

CHAPTER 6

Strategic Realignment:
Finding Clarity in the Cocoon

The cocoon stage is not just about change; it's about transformation. Just as the caterpillar dissolves completely before emerging as a butterfly, this stage requires breaking down old structures and reorganizing them into something entirely new. For leaders and entrepreneurs, this is a time of deep reflection and realignment, refining strategies, visions, and values. It is where misalignments are confronted, and clarity is reborn.

Strategic realignment is not a pause to reassess; it is an intentional process where every action, decision, and system is aligned with your long-term goals. This phase positions you to lead with greater focus, adaptability, and impact.

The Need for Strategic Realignment

Imagine taking a road trip without a map. You may have the best car and plenty of fuel, but you'll wander aimlessly without direction, wasting time and resources. Business is no different. Losing sight of your vision or failing to adapt to changed realities leads to frustration and inefficiency. Through strategic realignment, you ensure that your activities, values, and goals allow you to tackle challenges with confidence and purpose.

Reflection Activity:
- When was the last time you revisited your business strategy?
- Are the actions you're taking today helping to move you closer to your long-term vision?

You cannot realign until you know where you are. Strategic realignment begins with a candid inventory of your business's operations and your leadership style and mindset. Once you know where you are, you can chart a clear course forward.

Practical Exercise: Self-Assessment Checklist

Rate yourself or your business on a scale of 1–5 in the following areas:
1. Clarity of vision and goals.
2. Alignment of daily actions with long-term objectives.
3. Efficiency and effectiveness of current systems and processes.
4. Leadership adaptability and communication.
5. Personal fulfillment and work-life balance.

Reflection Activity:
- Which area received the lowest score?
- What is one step you can take today to begin improving it?

The Power of Reflection in the Cocoon Stage

Reflection is not about dwelling on mistakes; it is about learning from them. The cocoon phase gives space for insights to surface and clarity to take form. By asking yourself hard questions: What is working? What is not? What needs to change? You uncover the actions that truly align with your core visions and values.

Lessons from the Field: Real-Life Scenario

Tina: Revitalizing Growth Through Customer Connection

Tina's online boutique had taken off in a big way, fueled by her passion for edgy fashion and her talent for marketing. Orders flowed in, and her business flourished in its first year. However, over time, Tina's sales began to stagnate. The momentum that had propelled her boutique forward was fading, and she couldn't figure out why.

Frustrated but determined, Tina took a step back to regroup. She pored over her sales data, customer feedback, and marketing efforts in search of answers. What she discovered was startling: in her pursuit of new customers, she had unintentionally neglected her loyal ones—the very people who had supported her from the beginning. E-mails went unanswered; follow-ups were inconsistent, and there was no system in place to keep even her most dedicated customers engaged.

Armed with this insight, Tina set out to realign her strategy. She launched a loyalty program that rewarded repeat customers with points for every purchase made, redeemable against discounts or exclusive items. She also introduced personalized outreach, sending thank-you emails and early access to new products to her top customers. Lastly, she became more active on social media, engaging her community by soliciting feedback and ideas for upcoming product launches.

The results were immediate. Customers who had once felt overlooked returned enthusiastically, drawn by the renewed attention and exclusive perks. The loyalty program increased repeat business and fostered a sense of community among her customers. By prioritizing relationships, Tina reignited sales growth and built a more resilient foundation for her business.

Looking back, Tina realized that true transformation began with reflection. Shifting her focus from constant customer to meaningful connection allowed her to break through the plateau and create a far more sustainable business model. Today, her boutique thrives on the loyalty and trust of her dedicated customer base.

Key Takeaway: Tina's story highlights the power of reflection and realignment in business growth. Focus on nurturing existing relationships and align your actions with your goals to create meaningful growth and sustainable success.

Reflection Activity:

- Think of a time when reflection led to a breakthrough in your business or personal life.
- How do you create space for regular reflection in your routine?

Using Tools to Realign Strategically

Reflection is powerful, but it requires structure to be actionable. Here are three tools to help you realign strategically:

SWOT Analysis for Realignment:

Go back to your SWOT Analysis from Chapter 1. How has your business changed?

- Have your strengths changed or grown?
- Are there new opportunities or threats in your market?

The 5 Whys for Strategy:

Use the 5 Whys to find the root cause of a recurring problem.

Example: Low Employee Productivity
1. Why? Employees are not engaged.
2. Why? There is no clear communication about their role and responsibilities.
3. Why? Leaders have not provided clear expectations or consistent feedback.
4. Why? There is no formal process for team performance review or goal setting.
5. Why? Leaders have been focused on urgent tasks rather than strategic planning.

Root Cause: The lack of structured leadership planning has led to unclear expectations and poor engagement.

Action Plan:
- Develop a systematic performance review process, including regular one-on-ones.
- Hold quarterly strategic planning sessions to align team goals and organizational objectives.
- Train leaders in effective communication and delivery of effective feedback.

Mind Mapping for Vision Clarity

Create a mind map from your core vision, branching out to include goals, challenges, and potential solutions—this can help identify misalignments and highlight areas for growth and development.

Reflection Activity:
- Which tool resonates most with your current challenges?
- How can you use it to create actionable insights?

Reconnect to Your Why

Your "why" is the heart of your business, the driving force behind your journey, and the motivation that keeps you moving forward. However, the demands of daily operations can sometimes cause you to lose sight of it. Strategic realignment requires reconnecting with your purpose to ensure it remains relevant and aligned with your current vision and values.

Why Statement Exercise
1. Write down why you originally founded your business.
2. Reflect on how your purpose has evolved since then.
3. Rewrite your "why" to incorporate your current vision and values.

Example:
- Original Why: "To provide affordable fitness solutions for busy professionals."
- Evolved Why: "To empower professionals to prioritize wellness through accessible, personalized fitness plans."

Reflection Activity:
- Does your current "why" still inspire and motivate you?
- How can you integrate your purpose more fully into your daily actions?

Creating a Strategic Realignment Plan

After reflecting and assessing, take action. A strategic realignment plan provides a clear roadmap for addressing misalignments and moving forward with confidence.

Steps for Strategic Realignment:
1. Identify What Needs to Change: Highlight areas of misalignment or inefficiency.

2. Outline How You'll Change It: Develop specific steps and timelines for improvement.
3. Determine Who Will Be Involved: Identify team members, mentors, or external resources that can help.
4. Set Benchmarks for Success: Define measurable outcomes to track your progress.

Example Strategic Realignment Plan:

- Problem: Marketing strategies aren't bringing desired results.
- Solution: Invest in a data-driven approach, including customer feedback surveys and performance analytics.
- Timeline: Redesign campaigns within the next quarter.
- Success Benchmark: Achieve a 20% increase in customer engagement within six months.

Lessons from the Cocoon: Clarity is Power

The caterpillar's transformation is not random, it's intentional, guided by its DNA blueprint. Similarly, your strategic realignment is about reconnecting to your business's blueprint and ensuring every decision reflects your core vision and values.

Reflection Activity:

- What is one area in your business that feels "off"?
- How can realigning it bring you closer to your vision?

Key Takeaway: Transformation requires realignment. True growth is not about working harder; it's about working smarter. The time you invest in reflection, assessment, and realignment ensures that your efforts are intentional and bring you closer to your desired outcomes rather than leading you astray.

Call to Action: Start Realigning! Think about an area in your business or your leadership where something feels misaligned. What adjustments can you make to align it with your vision and goals?

- Choose one of the tools discussed in this chapter to start diagnosing the source of the problem.
- Commit to making one big change this week and monitor the outcome.

As your clarity deepens, your systems must evolve to support what comes next. Let's explore how to elevate your influence and lead from alignment.

CHAPTER 7

Expand Your Influence:
Direct with Clarity and Bonding

While the caterpillar works within its cocoon, its wings begin to form delicate yet powerful tools that will allow it to navigate the world in ways it could never have imagined. In many ways, influence is like wings: the ability to inspire, guide, and elevate others while propelling your leadership to new heights.

Leadership is not about authority; it's about connection. Influence is what empowers you to move people toward a shared vision, not through commands but through trust, authenticity, and collaboration. In this chapter, we will explore how to strengthen your influence through effective communication, relationship-building, and collaborative activities, ensuring that your transformation extends beyond yourself and creates a meaningful impact on others.

The Power of Influence in Leadership

Influence is the unseen force that mobilizes teams, spurs action, and delivers results. It's not about control or authority, it's earned through authenticity, empathy, and consistent actions that inspire others to trust and follow you. Whether you're leading a team, collaborating with clients, or engaging with stakeholders, influence is the foundation of effective leadership.

Reflection Activity:

- Think of a leader who deeply inspired or motivated you.
- What qualities made their influence impactful?
- How do those qualities manifest in your leadership?

Authenticity: The Foundation of Influence

Influence starts with authenticity. People are drawn toward leaders who are genuine, transparent and conform to their values. Authentic leaders command trust, the foundation of any meaningful relationship. When your actions are congruent with your words and values, you inspire others to follow you because they want to, not because they have to.

Lessons from the Field: Real-Life Scenario

Danielle: Embracing Authenticity to Lead with Impact

When Danielle was appointed chief executive of the family business, she felt that the role came with great expectations. Her father had founded the company through hard work for many years, and all the workers remained loyal to him. For Danielle, it felt like an uphill task stepping into his shoes. It didn't take long for her to face resistance, either. Some senior team members struggled to accept her as a leader, seeing her as too inexperienced and unproven. Doubts surfaced in whispered conversations, her authority was subtly dismissed, and workplace tension grew.

At first, Danielle was tempted to assert herself forcefully and demand the respect she felt she deserved. But deep down, she knew that approach did not align with who she was. Instead, she chose a different route, one rooted in authenticity. At her first all-staff meeting, Danielle addressed the team directly. She acknowledged the challenges of her new role and admitted she didn't have all the answers. Rather than positioning herself as an all-knowing leader, she invited the team to share their expertise and collaborate on solutions. "This business is as much yours as it is mine," she told them. "I want to learn from you and grow with you."

Her vulnerability elicited an unexpected response. Those employees who had been skeptical began to see her in a new light, not as a woman trying to replace her father, but as a leader with her own vision. She followed up with regular one-on-one meetings, where she listened to her team's concerns, valued their input, and acted on their feedback. She fostered a sense of shared purpose and commitment by setting clear goals and aligning their efforts with the company's long-term mission, creating a sense of purpose.

Over time, these efforts began to shift workplace dynamics. The very employees who initially resisted her leadership, especially the senior team members, became her strongest supporters, rallying behind her vision for the company's future. Danielle earned the respect and trust she had sought not by asserting her authority but by leading with authenticity and genuine connection.

Today, under Danielle's leadership, the family business is thriving. She often looks back and reflects on how embracing vulnerability and fostering real relationships transformed a difficult beginning into a powerful leadership journey. For Danielle, authenticity wasn't just a strategy; it was the foundation for her success.

Key Takeaway: Danielle's story proves that authenticity is a leader's greatest asset. Leaders who are honest, transparent, and willing to connect with others can build trust, align their teams, and inspire lasting loyalty.

Practical Exercise: Authentic Leadership Assessment
1. Take a moment to reflect on your interactions over the past week.
   - Were your actions in line with your values?
   - When you were challenged, did you lead with transparency and candor?
2. Name one area where you would like to fully embody your authentic self in the next leadership moment.

Reflection Activity:
- How does bringing your authentic self to the leadership table enhance your relationship with your team or customers?

How to Have Conversations That Inspire Action

Influence is achieved through powerful, clear communication. Leadership is less about speaking and more about listening, understanding, and collaboratively forging a path forward.

The Three Pillars of Leadership Communication

1. Clarity: Share expectations, goals, and feedback.
2. Empathy: Listen to understand, not just to reply. Show appreciation for others' points of view.
3. Inspiration: Use stories, vision, and encouragement to unify and motivate your team.

The Storytelling Framework

Storytelling is one of the most powerful ways to inspire action. Write a story that connects your audience to your vision:

1. Introduction: Set up the challenge or goal.
2. Body: Describe the efforts, struggles, or turning points along the way.
3. Conclusion: Highlight the resolution and what was learned.

Example Story:

When we launched this product for the first time, we were full of excitement but lacked direction. We had a beautiful offering, but we were speaking to everyone and reaching no one. The first month was quiet. Embarrassingly quiet. Orders trickled in, and self-doubt started to creep in. I questioned whether the idea had been worth it or whether I had missed something obvious that others could see.

Instead of panicking, we paused. I reached out to a few trusted customers and asked what resonated, what didn't, and what they truly needed. The feedback was honest and humbling. We had focused so much on features that we forgot to tell the story, the "why" behind the product. It wasn't just about selling a thing. It was about helping people feel something: seen, supported, aligned.

We shifted our messaging. We led with the problem it solved and the transformation it offered. I shared more of my personal journey and the story behind why this product was born in the first place. Within three weeks of that pivot, sales increased by 40%, engagement doubled, and more importantly, the messages we received changed. People didn't just want to buy, they felt connected.

That's when I truly understood: clarity isn't just about what you offer. It's about how you make people feel. Storytelling bridges that gap.

Reflection Activity:
- How can you use storytelling to inspire your team or clients?
- What story from your own journey could create a meaningful connection?

Building Trust: The Currency of Influence

Trust is the foundation of influence. Without it, teams falter, relationships weaken, and leadership loses its impact. Building trust takes consistent actions, clear communication, and unwavering integrity.

Building Trust as a Leader
1. Consistency: Deliver on promises and follow through on commitments.
2. Transparency: Share both successes and challenges openly.
3. Empowerment: Allow team members to take ownership of their work.

Reflection Activity:
- What have you done recently to establish trust in your team or with your clients?
- What's one area you'd like to improve the dynamics of trust?

Nurture Collaboration and Connection

Influence is most powerful when leaders cultivate collaboration and create environments where diverse perspectives are not just welcomed but valued. True collaboration isn't about forcing agreement, it's about aligning different viewpoints toward a shared goal.

Lessons from the Field: Real-Life Scenario

David: Bridging Gaps to Spark Collaboration and Creativity

The marketing director for a fast-growing company, David took pride in leading a team of talented professionals. His department was composed of two core teams: the creative team, responsible for designing compelling campaigns, and the analytics team, tasked with measuring performance and refining strategies. While the teams excelled in their respective roles, David noticed a growing disconnect between them. Meetings often became tense, with the creative team rejecting data-based recommendations as restrictive, while the analytics team criticized the creatives for being too "abstract" and disconnected from measurable outcomes.

That wasn't just a personality clash; it was starting to impact departmental performance. Campaigns lacked cohesion, deadlines were missed, and results fell far short of expectations. Realizing that both teams brought valued perspectives yet struggled to communicate, David knew he had to act. Determined to bridge the gap, he set out to cultivate an environment where collaboration could thrive.

David brought in regular brainstorming sessions that both teams were required to attend together. The sessions were not about critiquing each other's work but about sharing their unique approaches and finding a way to align them. To set the tone, David opened the first session with a simple yet powerful team exercise: each team member had to share one strength they brought to the table and one area where they could use support. This exercise shifted the dynamic, helping the teams see each other as collaborators rather than competitors.

Over time, the sessions produced remarkable results. The creative team began incorporating data insights into their storytelling, creating emotionally compelling and strategically targeted campaigns. Meanwhile, the analytics team developed a deeper appreciation for the power of narrative and became more flexible in their approach to data interpretation. One campaign, in particular, combined the creative team's bold visuals with the analytics team's deep understanding of customer behavior, resulting in the company's most successful product launch to date.

For David, the breakthrough wasn't just about improving campaign results; it was about creating a culture fostering mutual respect and collaboration. He brought the teams closer together, ensuring that every individual felt their contribution mattered. This transformation turned a divided department into a cohesive unit that now thrived on collective success.

Key Takeaway: David's story evidences the power of collaboration in leadership. When a leader creates avenues for dialogue and unites diverse perspectives, it unlocks innovative solutions and builds stronger, more unified teams.

Practical Exercise: Stakeholder Mapping
1. Choose an ongoing or upcoming project.
2. List all the stakeholders.
3. Map their roles, views, and how their contributions relate to the objective.
4. Meet with stakeholders to align efforts and ignite collaboration.

Reflection Activity:

- How might you create more space for collaboration with your team?
- What actions can you take to align stakeholders around a shared vision?

The Use of Influence to Manage Conflict

Conflict tests a leader's credibility but also provides an opportunity to earn greater respect and trust by handling it wisely and fairly. Leaders who manage conflict effectively gain confidence in their ability to guide others through challenges.

On-the-Job Tips for Handling Conflict
1. Listen with Interest: Approach conflict with a goal to understand and not judge.
2. Focus on the Problem and Not the Person: Make solutions the focus of the discussion.
3. Seek Win-Win Solutions: Seek solutions that work for everyone involved.

Real-Life Example:

Conflict: Two team members were at odds over project priorities. One advocated for a long-term creative solution that was in line with the company vision, while the other focused on an immediate and resource-efficient approach. Their disagreement quickly escalated into tension in meetings, dragging down morale and productivity across the rest of the team.

Resolution: Realizing the increasing strife, the leader stepped in, looking at the conflict not as a failure but as an opportunity for clarity and alignment. He began by scheduling one-on-one meetings with each team member, giving them the opportunity to voice their concerns. During the meetings, the leader practiced active listening, paraphrasing each person's concerns to ensure they felt understood and respected.

Next, the leader organized a collaborative team discussion. At the start of the meeting, he reframed the issue by relating it to the bigger goals of the project. Using storytelling, he reminded the team of their shared mission and emphasized how their collective success depended on unified efforts. This approach set a neutral and inspiring tone.

The leader then facilitated a compromise by guiding the conversation toward a solution that incorporated both perspectives. He illustrated how the creative solution could serve as a foundation for long-term value while integrating with the resource-efficient approach to meet the immediate deliverables. Together, they developed a phased plan that incorporated elements of both ideas, ensuring that each team member felt valued for their contribution.

Impact: The compromise resolved not only the visible conflict at the moment but also nurtured an attitude of respect and collaboration. The leader's composure and empathetic approach set a powerful example for future conflict resolution, improving team dynamics. After the resolution, both team members reported better cooperation, stronger relationships, and an outcome that exceeded everybody's expectations.

Key Takeaway: Leadership in conflict requires empathy, reframing, and collaboration. Leaders who actively listen, align the team around shared goals, and seek solutions that benefit all can transform discord into an opportunity for growth and innovation.

Reflection Activity:

- How might you begin to reframe conflict as an opportunity to bring people closer together?

Lessons from the Cocoon: Influence is Transformation in Action

The caterpillar doesn't grow wings just to see the world from a different perspective; it grows wings to interact with the world in a completely new way. Similarly, as a leader, your influence isn't about you; it's about empowering others to grow, collaborate, and achieve. Influence is a transformation in action.

Reflection Activity:

1. Think of one person you lead or work with.
2. Jot down three ways you can elevate their experience or contribute to their development this week.
3. Commit to doing one of those things today.

Key Take Away: Influence is the Wings of the Leader

Influence isn't about control, it's about connection. When you embrace authenticity, communicate powerfully, and build trust, you equip yourself with wings to inspire others and create a meaningful impact. With influence, you can unite people to work toward a shared purpose and elevate everyone involved.

Call to Action: Increase Your Influence

1. Take a moment to reflect on what authenticity, communication, and trust look like in your leadership today.
2. Identify a specific area to improve and make a plan to take action in that area this week.
3. Commit to building influence through connection, not authority.

Now that you've grounded your influence and clarified your communication, you're ready for transformation in action. In the next chapter, we move from insight to implementation, where your vision begins to take flight.

PART 3

The Ascent: Leading, Implementing, and Rising with Intention

The Butterfly Stage

You've done the inner work and the time has finally come. This next stage is about movement, implementing what you've designed with confidence, clarity, and aligned momentum.

The butterfly has emerged from its cocoon, its wings unfolding for the very first time. What was once confined to the safety of a branch now takes flight, experiencing the world from a newfound strength and perspective. The transformation is complete, not just because the butterfly has changed, but because it now operates by using what it has become.

The Butterfly Stage represents implementation and re-emergence. It's the stage where everything learned and refined during the Caterpillar and Cocoon Stages culminates in a surge of action. Strategies become systems; ideas take shape, and vision transforms into reality. But this phase is not merely about doing, it is about becoming. It embodies transformation, embracing a new capacity to lead, grow, and inspire.

The Duality of the Butterfly Stage

The Butterfly Stage integrates two vital aspects of growth:

Personal Re-emergence: This is the moment when your internal transformation becomes visible to others. The confidence, clarity, and resilience you've cultivated now shine through in your leadership and relationships.

Strategic Implementation: This is where plans turn into action. The strategies and systems you've developed are now implemented, driving measurable outcomes and fostering sustainable success.

Visualize This: Imagine the butterfly stretching its wings for the first time. With each flap, it lifts itself higher, embracing new opportunities and perspectives. Similarly, with every choice and action in this phase of your journey, you put yourself one step closer to the heights you have worked so diligently to reach.

A Time for Action and Impact

The Butterfly Stage is more than just achieving goals; it is about fully embracing your presence in the world. Implementation isn't merely about action; it's about acting with intention, alignment, and vision. It's about creating a ripple effect, where your transformation inspires and empowers others to evolve with you.

Reflection Activity:

- What strengths have emerged within you during the Caterpillar and Cocoon Stages?
- How do you leverage these strengths to lead with more impact and purpose?

What You'll Explore in this Phase

The Butterfly Phase is where transformation meets action. In the next several chapters you'll learn:

Chapter 8: Action-Based Leadership – Shifting strategy to execution, with focus and accountability.

Chapter 9: Systems for Sustainability – Building the structures that keep you successful in the long haul.

Chapter 10: Thriving in Balance – Integrating personal and professional fulfillment to sustain your growth.

Chapter 11: Leading Others into Flight - Extend your leadership by creating the conditions for others to grow, thrive, and take flight within the systems you've designed.

Key Takeaway: The Butterfly Stage is your time to emerge fully. By implementing your strategies and embodying your transformation, you're not just experiencing change, you're leading it. This phase is a powerful reminder that transformation isn't complete until it's lived.

Call to Action: As you step into the Butterfly Stage, take time to reflect on how far you have come. What personal and professional growth have you experienced? What small yet significant action will you take today to step fully into this new phase?

CHAPTER 8

Action-Oriented Leadership: The Development of the Vision

Transformation requires action. A cocoon might mark the beginning of the butterfly's transformation, but only by flapping its new wings does the butterfly gain the strength to fly. The same applies to leadership: your ideas and vision come to life through deliberate, focused action. Action-centered leadership bridges the intention-impact gap. It's not just about executing plans but also about fostering accountability and cultivating a culture of excellence within your organization.

Leadership is not measured by how many ideas you generate but by how many you make real. Action-oriented leaders do not wait for perfect conditions; they prioritize progress over perfection, taking consistent steps forward and adapting along the way.

Principles of Action-Oriented Leadership

At its core, action-based leadership is about courage, decisiveness, and execution. It is the ability to move forward with conviction, even when uncertainty lies ahead, and inspire others to follow your lead. The best leaders balance action with embracing learning from mistakes or setbacks.

Reflection Activity:
- Think of a time when you delayed taking action.
- What held you back?

- How would acting decisively have changed the outcome?

From Vision to Execution: Bridging the Gap

Great visions often falter without equally great execution. Turning vision into reality requires a clear roadmap, consistent effort, and the courage to take risks. Execution is where strategy meets momentum. It's about taking the first step and building on it until your vision becomes tangible.

Practical Exercise: Turning Vision into Goals
1. Write down your current big idea or vision.
2. Identify three actionable objectives that can be accomplished within the next six months.
3. Break each objective into specific tasks or milestones.
4. Assign deadlines to each task to stay on track.

Sample Example:
- Vision: Introduce a new product line.
  - Objective 1: Conduct market research.
    - Activity: Survey 100 potential customers.
    - Deadline: 2 weeks.
  - Objective 2: Finalize product design.
    - Activity: Meet with the design team.
    - Deadline: 1 month.
  - Objective 3: Launch marketing campaign.
    - Activity: Design ad materials.
    - Deadline: 6 weeks.

The Courage to Decide

Leadership is rooted in action, often without having complete information. Waiting for perfect clarity can lead to stagnation, while bold, informed decision-making generates momentum and opens new possibilities. Effective leaders know that smart risk-taking and course correction are integral to the process, ensuring adaptability and sustained progress.

Lessons from the Field: Real-Life Scenario

Jasmine: Bold Leadership in the Face of Crisis

Jasmine had poured everything into building her tech startup. Her team was small but dedicated, and early success had fueled their optimism. But as the company scaled, challenges mounted. A series of unexpected setbacks delayed client payments, and a sudden spike in operational costs left the company strapped for cash. Jasmine faced a difficult choice: scale back operations to conserve resources or take a bold risk by launching a new product ahead of schedule.

The product, a cutting-edge SaaS tool that had been in development for months, held great promise. Her team was confident of its potential, but an early launch carried risks. Technical issues or market indifference could spell disaster, yet scaling back felt like surrender. Standing at the crossroads, Jasmine bore the weight of a decision that could define her company's future.

Rather than letting fear paralyze her, Jasmine relied on her leadership instincts. She gathered her team for an all-hands meeting, openly laid out the options, and invited their input. Her engineers assured her the product was almost ready; her marketing lead urged her to move quickly before competitors released similar tools. Jasmine's customer survey data revealed strong demand for the product's features.

Armed with this insight, Jasmine made her decision: the product launch would proceed, albeit at a calculated risk. Her team rallied behind her working tirelessly to finalize development and execute a targeted marketing campaign. Jasmine herself took an active role in hosting webinars and leveraging industry connections to generate buzz about the product.

The launch was a resounding success. Early adopters gave glowing reviews, new clients flooded in, and the revenue influx stabilized the company's cash flow. More importantly, the move reinforced the company's reputation as an industry innovator. Looking back, Jasmine realized that bold, decisive action rooted in collaboration and data had transformed a crisis into opportunity and growth.

Key Takeaway: Jasmine's story shows that leadership requires making tough decisions. She revitalized her company and positioned it for long-term success by engaging her team, analyzing data, and taking calculated risks.

Practical Exercise: Decision-Making Framework
1. Define the Problem: Clearly articulate the issue at hand.
2. Identify Alternatives: Enumerate possible courses of action or solutions
3. Weigh Risks and Benefits: Weigh the potential outcomes for each alternative
4. Make a decision: Set a specific time to make a decision and stick with it
5. Reflect and Adjust: Review the outcome and make necessary adjustments

Establishing a Culture of Accountability

Action-based leadership is not about personal performance; it's about fostering accountability within your team. When accountability is embedded in a company's culture, team members gain a clear understanding of their roles and responsibilities, ensuring collective progress toward shared goals.

Tips to Create Accountability
1. Define Expectations: Clearly communicate roles and responsibilities.
2. Set Measurable Objectives: Set specific, time-bound goals
3. Provide Regular Feedback: Give direction and celebrate milestones
4. Model Accountability: Lead by example by keeping your commitments.

Reflection Activity:
- How are you currently holding yourself and your team accountable?
- What's one step you can take to strengthen accountability within your organization?

Overcoming the Fear of Failure

One of the most significant blockages to taking action is fear of failure. However, successful leaders recognize that failure is not the opposite of success; it's an essential part of the journey. By reframing failure as feedback, leaders approach challenges with curiosity and resilience, continuously learning and improving with each attempt.

Practical Exercise: Failure Reflection Framework
1. Write down a recent failure or setback.

2. Answer the following questions:
   - What did I learn from this experience?
   - How am I going to apply this lesson to get better at my next action?
3. Write down one step you will take to move forward.

Example Reflection:
- Failure: A marketing campaign performed below expectations
- Lesson Learned: Messaging wasn't effective with the target audience
- Next Step: Conduct surveys with the audience before the next campaign launch.

Inspiring Action in Others

Leadership is not about acting alone but inspiring others to take urgent, purposeful, aligned actions. Great leaders communicate a clear vision, build trust, and empower their teams to take ownership of their responsibilities, driving meaningful progress together.

Lessons from the Field: Real-Life Scenario

Martin: Reviving a Team with Vision and Purpose

As head of the product development team in his company, Martin had always taken pride in the talent and dedication that defined his colleagues. However, he recently noticed a troubling shift. Missed deadlines, dwindling enthusiasm, and brainstorming sessions that had lost their spark. Once dynamic and engaging, these meetings now felt stale and uninspired. Low morale was seeping into every aspect of the team, and Martin knew that if things didn't change soon, the company's goals would be at risk.

Determined to change this, Martin took a step back and began to reflect on his leadership. In his relentless focus on deliverables and deadlines, he had lost sight of something crucial: connecting the team's daily efforts to the company's larger mission. His team wasn't just disengaged from their tasks, they had lost sight of the meaning behind their work. Recognizing this, Martin decided to take action.

He called a team meeting, but this time it was different. Instead of the usual discussion of performance metrics and project updates, Martin began with a story. In vivid detail, he painted a picture of the company's vision: what they were striving to innovate and whose lives their work would impact for the better. He connected their roles to that mission, illustrating how their efforts contributed to something far more significant than just completing tasks. "What you do here," he said, "isn't just about meeting deadlines, it's about shaping something meaningful, something that truly matters."

But Martin didn't stop there. Over the next week, he met with each of the team members individually. He took time to discuss their strengths, acknowledge their unique contributions, and set personal goals. He also invited their input on how they could collaborate more effectively. By making each of them feel seen and valued, Martin reignited their sense of purpose and ownership, restoring the passion that had once defined their team.

The results were transformative: the renewed sense of purpose ignited a surge in creativity and productivity. Brainstorming sessions became energetic again; collaboration flourished, and the team began producing some of their best work. One project.

which had been stalled for weeks, was not only completed ahead of schedule but exceeded expectations.

In retrospect, Martin realized that leadership was not just about managing tasks, it was about inspiring people. He created an environment where they could thrive by reconnecting his team's efforts to the company's mission and recognizing their unique contributions.

Key Takeaway: Martin's story highlights a powerful lesson: the importance of connecting people to purpose. When leaders articulate a clear vision and acknowledge each individual's role in achieving it, they can reignite motivation, spark creativity, and drive meaningful results.

Practical Exercise: How to Empower Your Team
1. Communicate a Clear Vision: Share the "why" behind the work.
2. Define Roles and Responsibilities: Clearly articulate how each team member contributes to the goal.
3. Follow-up: Check progress regularly, offer support, and celebrate milestones.

Lessons from the Butterfly: Action Fuels Flight

A butterfly does not hesitate to use its wings. It flaps them repeatedly, strengthening them for flight. In the same way, leaders must embrace action as the catalyst for growth. Every step, whether it's a success or a setback, lays the foundation for future success.

Reflection Activity:
1. Write down one project or goal for which you've felt hesitant to act.

2. Write down three small, immediate steps you can take to move it forward.
3. Commit to taking the first step within 24 hours.

Key Takeaway: Leadership is Action in Motion

Action-oriented leadership turns vision into results. By taking confident steps, fostering accountability, and inspiring your team, you will ensure that your business and your leadership continue evolving and growing.

Call to Action: Take the First Step
1. Identify one thing, project, or decision you have been putting off.
2. List three concrete actions to get it moving.
3. Commit to taking the first step today, no matter how small.

You've clarified the what—now it's time to implement the how. Let's build the systems that will carry your leadership and operations forward with consistency.

CHAPTER 9

Thriving as a Leader:
Achieving Balance and Excellence

The butterfly's flight depends on balance. Its delicate wings must work in perfect harmony to move forward. In the same way, thriving as a leader requires balance: vision and execution, work and life, ambition and well-being.

This chapter explores how to cultivate a thriving mindset, avoid burnout, and lead with resilience and purpose. Thriving is not just about what you achieve; it's about how you achieve it with alignment, intention, and sustainability.

The Myth of Perfect Balance

Balance is not about perfection; it's about alignment. Too often, leaders chase the illusion of "having it all" only to end up overwhelmed and unfulfilled. True thriving does not mean doing everything, it means focusing on what really matters and aligning your time, energy, and actions with your core values and priorities.

Reflection Activity:
- How do you currently define balance in your life and leadership?
- Are your priorities in line with that definition?

What Thriving Looks Like for a Leader

Thriving is more than survival, it's leading with energy, clarity, and intention. Thriving leaders create rhythms in their lives that sustain both personal growth and professional success.

Key Characteristics of Thriving Leaders
1. Energy Management: They understand their limits and know how to recharge when needed.
2. Values-Driven: Their actions consistently reflect their values and goals.
3. Empathy and Connection: They develop solid relationships with their teams, clients, and communities.

Reflection Activity:
- How are these qualities reflected in your own leadership?
- How might you strengthen one area that is a weakness for you?

How to Integrate Work and Life

Balance is not achieved by rigidly separating work and life but by integrating them in a sustainable and fulfilling way. By aligning your daily actions with your personal and professional priorities, you build a life that supports your well-being and ambitions.

Lessons from the Field: Real-Life Scenario

Angela: From Overwhelmed to Empowered (Balance)

Angela's nonprofit had grown beyond her wildest dreams. What had begun as a small organization, meeting the community's needs had developed into a well-respected organization that made meaningful changes in the lives of so many. But with growth came increased demands, and Angela, as founder and leader, felt responsible for every detail. Her calendar was packed with back-to-back meetings, funding pitches, team check-ins, and critical operational decisions. Her phone buzzed constantly and emails poured in faster than she could respond.

Angela's personal life began to suffer. She rarely had time to sit down for dinner with her family, her hobbies fell by the wayside, and even the simplest self-care routines felt like luxuries she couldn't afford. One evening, as she sat behind her desk staring blankly at yet another overwhelming to-do list, Angela realized she was on the brink of burnout. The mission she had worked hard to build and poured her heart into was consuming her.

Determined to do something different, Angela took a step back and reflected. First, she mapped out how she was spending her time and realized that many of her tasks could easily be delegated. Second, she admitted to herself that her lack of boundaries was unsustainable. From this reflection came two key decisions.

First, she set firm limits to her working day. She committed to ending her workday by 6 PM, reserving the evenings for family, relaxation, and personal time. Angela empowered her team by delegating operational tasks and project management responsibilities to make this possible. She trained her staff to take ownership of specific tasks, allowing her to focus on strategic leadership and big-picture planning, the work that required her expertise.

The transformation was almost magical: with her evenings free, Angela reconnected with her family and rediscovered her love for gardening. She arrived at work each day with energy and focus. Her team embraced their added responsibilities growing more efficient and confident in their roles. As a result, the nonprofit ran more smoothly than ever, achieving more significant impact without its founder needing to be involved in every detail.

Looking back, Angela often says that setting boundaries wasn't a personal decision; it was a leadership decision. In her quest for balance, she became more present, creative, and effective as a leader. Her organization's success did not diminish when she stepped back; in fact, it thrived because she allowed her team to step up.

Key Takeaway: Angela's story shows that balance is essential to sustainable leadership. By setting boundaries and entrusting her team with greater responsibilities, she not only protected her well-being but also empowered those around her to grow and succeed.

Practical Tips for Work-Life Integration:
1. Set Boundaries: Establish a clear distinction between work and personal time, and respect those boundaries.
2. Delegate Wisely: Allow your team to take ownership of tasks that do not need your direct involvement.
3. Schedule Personal Time: Make self-care, family time, and hobbies non-negotiable.

Reflection Activity:
- Write down three areas where your work-life integration could improve.
- List one actionable step for each area (e.g., delegating a task, scheduling weekly family time).

The Danger of Burnout

Burnout is one of the most significant threats to a leader's ability to succeed. It saps your energy, clouds judgment, and impacts relationships, creating a vicious cycle of stress and diminishing returns. Recognizing and addressing burnout is critical for sustained success.

Signs of Burnout
- Chronic fatigue or lack of motivation.
- Decreased productivity or creativity.
- Feeling detached or cynical about your work.

Practical Exercise: Burnout Recovery Plan
1. Identify one activity or habit that drains your energy.
2. Replace it with a restorative practice, such as meditation, exercise, or time with loved ones.
3. Schedule at least one "recharge" activity into your weekly routine.

Reflection Activity:
- What is one habit or practice you can implement today to combat burnout?

Thriving Through Resilience

Thriving leaders don't shy away from challenges; they embrace them as learning opportunities. Resilience is what allows you to adjust, learn, and keep moving forward when things don't go as planned.

Lessons from the Field: Real-Life Scenario

Raj: Turning Loss into a Comeback

Raj had poured everything into the tech startup he founded, and for years, the business grew steadily. Then in an instant, he lost his biggest client, a cornerstone revenue source, with a single phone call. Financially, it was a devastating blow; emotionally, it was even more so. Raj felt he had let his team down and began to question whether his firm could ever recover. The sense of defeat cast a long shadow, threatening to erode his confidence as a leader.

For days, Raj found himself trapped in a cycle of self-doubt, replaying the situation in his head. But he also knew that staying in this mindset would not help. So, he took a step back and reflected on what had gone wrong. Raj gathered the leadership team and conducted a post-mortem analysis of why the client had left. What they uncovered was a hard truth: the company's offerings had become too broad, diluting the personalized, proactive service that had once set them apart.

Taking that loss as an opportunity, rather than a setback, Raj refocused and realigned his business. He and his team worked to streamline their offerings, specializing in serving mid-sized tech companies, a niche they had excelled in before. Raj also implemented a new client relationship strategy, assigning dedicated account managers to provide personalized support and ensure proactive communication. With this refined approach, his team gained clarity and purpose, and they were determined to rebuild the company's reputation.

Months later, Raj's persistence paid off. His company secured two new contracts with clients who appreciated the special, high-touch service his team now offered. These new relationships not only compensated for the lost revenue but also positioned the company on a stronger, more sustainable path. Raj realized that the loss of that client, while painful, had been a turning point, a catalyst for transformation that made his business more focused and competitive.

Key Takeaway: Raj's story highlights the importance of resilience and adaptability in leadership. By reflecting on setbacks and using them as opportunities to sharpen your approach, you can emerge stronger and more aligned with your goals.

Tips to Build Resilience:
1. Practice Gratitude: Always celebrate the victories, and acknowledge the progress, no matter how small.
2. Build a Support Network: Lean on mentors, peers, or loved ones for guidance and encouragement.
3. Focus on Solutions: Move from dwelling on the problems to finding actionable steps.

Reflection Activity:
- How do you currently respond to setbacks?
- What is one way you can build resilience in your leadership?

Creating a Thriving Culture in Your Organization

Thriving isn't an individual sport; it's a collective one. By creating a culture of balance, well-being, and growth within your organization, you empower your team to perform at their best.

Strategies for Creating a Culture of Thriving:
1. Encourage Flexibility: Provide arrangements like working from home or flexible working hours.
2. Recognize Successes: Regularly recognize both big and small successes.
3. Grow People: Invest in learning, growth, and professional development opportunities.

Practical Exercise: Well-being Check-In with Your Team
1. Schedule a well-being-focused check-in with your team.

2. Ask each team member to share one thing that helps them thrive and one thing that they need support for.
3. From the feedback collected, identify changes in the work environment that should be made to support balance and productivity.

Lessons from the Butterfly: Thriving is a Process

A butterfly's flight isn't a straight line, it dances with the wind, adapting to its environment with poise and resilience. Similarly, thriving as a leader is a continuing process of adjustment, growth, and realignment. Thriving doesn't mean achieving perfection; it means living and leading in alignment with your values and priorities.

Reflection Activity:
1. Write down one area of your life where you feel "off-balance."
2. Name three small steps you can take this week to realign an area of your life or work.
3. Come back to this list weekly to check your progress.

Key Takeaway: Thriving Leaders Lead with Intention. It isn't about getting it all done; it's about creating a life and running a business that reflects your values, priorities, and well-being. By balancing ambition with sustainability, resilience with self-care, and connection with purpose, you build a strong foundation for lasting success and fulfillment.

Call to Action: Thrive On
1. Identify one area of your life or leadership you'd like to start improving this week.
2. Do this: Take a step – set a boundary, practice gratitude, or delegate – just one step.

3. Notice the shift in energy, effectiveness, and sense of balance.

Once the systems are in place, your next step is learning to thrive within them, without losing sight of balance, clarity, or fulfillment.

CHAPTER 10

Business and Leadership in Harmony: Creating Synergy for Success

As the butterfly takes flight, its wings work in complete harmony, carrying it toward new opportunities. Each wing moves in precision, complementing the other, creating both balance and momentum. In leadership and business, this synergy is between two fundamental forces: inspired leadership and operational excellence. Each of these combines to create synergy, which fuels growth, adaptability, and sustainability.

This chapter is about aligning your personal development as a leader with your business's systems and processes. When leadership vision and operational systems are in harmony, they form a feedback loop in which the leader empowers the business, and the business, in turn, empowers the leader.

The Importance of Harmony

No business can thrive on systems alone, nor can it thrive solely on a leader's vision. Success depends on the synergy between the two. Effective leadership offers guidance and inspiration, while well-designed systems ensure execution and sustainability. Together, they create a foundation that adapts, evolves, and endures.

Reflection Activity:
- Is your current leadership style strengthening your business systems?
- Are your business systems supporting or holding back your personal development?

The Interplay of Business and Leadership

Leadership is a business's soul; its systems are its backbone. Together, they create a solid yet adaptable framework, resilient in the face of challenges and agile in seizing opportunities.

Lessons from the Field: Real-Life Scenario

Mia: Aligning Systems to Support Innovation

Mia's skincare brand was built on a simple yet powerful premise: creating high-quality, natural products that prioritized wellness and sustainability. Her innovative formulations and mission-driven promise quickly gained traction, and within a year, her small business had blossomed into a beloved name in the beauty industry. However, as demand grew, cracks in her operations began to show.

The turning point came during a holiday promotion that brought in an overwhelming surge of orders. Her team struggled to keep up, leading to shipping delays that frustrated customers and inventory shortages that caused backorders. Mia found herself stretched thin. Tracking inventory, managing customer complaints, and overseeing production all pulled her away from what she loved most, creating new products. It became clear that the lack of streamlined systems was holding her back and threatening her hard-earned reputation.

Determined to find a solution, Mia reflected on where her business was faltering. She finally realized the hands-on approach to managing every aspect of the company was no longer sustainable. Determined to regain control, she resolved to implement changes that would bring stability and allow her to lead more effectively.

At the top of her list was inventory management software which streamlined stock tracking and ensured that raw materials and finished products were always available when needed. Next, Mia brought in an operations manager, a step she had put off for months for fear of giving up control. By entrusting operational details to an experienced professional with experience in that area, Mia shifted her focus to innovation and strategy, strengthening her business for the long term.

The results were transformative: orders were processed faster, customer complaints dropped significantly, and her team was far more efficient. Freed from the day-to-day chaos, Mia went back to her creative roots and developed new product lines that wowed her customers and expanded her brand's reach. The systems she put into place didn't just solve her immediate problems but laid the foundation for sustainable growth.

Looking back, Mia learned that leadership is not about doing it all by yourself; rather, it's about creating the systems and empowering others to make your vision thrive. She positioned her brand for long-term success by aligning her operational backbone with her innovative leadership.

Key Takeaway: Mia's story shows that leadership vision must be aligned with business systems. Leaders who are all about harmony between innovation and operational efficiency will unleash their business's real potential.

Reflection Activity:
- Where might systems better support your leadership vision in your own business?
- What operational inefficiencies are sapping your strength as a leader?

Business Systems that Align with Your Leadership Goals

For harmony to exist, business systems must reflect the objectives and values of your leadership. Every process, decision, and action should move closer toward your vision so that your business runs as an extension of you and your leadership.

Practical Exercise: System Alignment Audit
1. Write down three important goals for your business.
2. For each goal, identify the systems currently in place to support it.
3. Assess whether these systems align with your vision and values.
4. Identify one system to improve or create.

Example:
- Goal: Improve customer satisfaction.
- System: Implement a CRM to track customer interactions and feedback.
- Action: Research and invest in CRM software within the next month.

Reflection Activity:
- How well do your current systems reflect your leadership values?

- What is one system you can refine to better support your goals?

Leveraging Leadership to Strengthen Systems

As a leader, you set the tone and direction for your business systems. By prioritizing clarity, consistency, and communication, you empower your team to execute effectively while maintaining alignment with your vision.

Tips for Strengthening Systems Through Leadership:
1. Clarity: Ensure everyone understands their roles and responsibilities.
2. Consistency: Regularly review and refine processes to maintain quality and efficiency.
3. Communication: Open lines of feedback and collaboration.

Scenario: Breakdown in the Sales Process

Issue: The sales process was difficult for employees to follow.

Remedy: The workshop will clarify expectations, provide a step-by-step walkthrough, and address any questions.

Reflection Question:
- How can you demonstrate leadership in clarifying and enhancing business systems?

Managing Growth vs Sustainability

Rapid growth can be exciting, but without sustainable practices, it will only lead to overwhelm and instability. Aligning leadership with systems harmonizes growth, making it intentional and manageable for long-term success.

Lessons from the Field: Real-Life Scenario

RAJ: Building Systems to Sustain Rapid Growth

Raj's tech startup had been a labor of love, and after years of hard work, his efforts were finally paying off. A big funding round had given him the resources to grow his team and scale the business. Raj was excited about his fast growth, bringing in new talent to take on bigger projects and meeting increasing client demands. But as the team grew, so did the challenges.

Without clear systems in place, the rapid expansion created chaos: deadlines were missed, communication between departments broke down, and team members grew frustrated by unclear roles and responsibilities. Projects that had previously been completed with ease now dragged on, frustrating clients and damaging the company's reputation. Instead of leading his team, Raj found himself constantly putting out fires. He knew something had to change.

Realizing the problem wasn't the team, but the lack of structure, Raj took a step back to assess how his business was operating. He saw that his startup's systems were still designed for a small team, even though the company had doubled in size. Determined to build a stronger foundation, Raj shifted his focus to creating the operational backbone his business needed.

First, he implemented project management tools to enhance team visibility and accountability. He introduced structured workflows with clearly defined roles, and set timelines and key milestones for each project. Raj also prioritized regular check-ins allowing teams to address bottlenecks and stay aligned with overall objectives. Additionally, he embraced delegation empowering his managers to take ownership of their teams while he focused on strategy and growth.

The impact was transformative. Project management tools fostered collaboration and helped teams meet deadlines with confidence and clarity. Once overwhelmed, the employees thrived under the streamlined workflows, and company projects gained momentum. Clients took notice, praising the improved communication and timely deliveries.

Looking back, Raj realized growth wasn't just about expanding the team but about creating an environment where people could thrive. By aligning strong leadership with effective systems, he prevented his start-up from burning out and also positioned it for long-term success.

Key Takeaway: Raj's story is a testament to the fact that rapid growth requires a deliberate well-structured foundation. By implementing systems that support your team and align with your vision, you can create a sustainable environment in which people and projects can genuinely thrive.

Practical Exercise: Growth Sustainability Plan
1. Identify one area of growth (e.g., expanding your team or launching a new product).
2. Outline the systems and resources needed to support this growth.
3. Set milestones to track progress and sustainability.

Building an Alignment Culture

Alignment does not stop with systems; it extends to fostering a culture where values, goals, and actions are seamlessly integrated. An alignment-driven culture empowers your team to work cohesively, driving mutual success.

How to Build an Alignment Culture

1. Shared Vision: Communicate the vision consistently to keep your team aligned and motivated.
2. Empowerment: Encourage team members to take ownership of their roles and responsibilities.
3. Alignment Check-Ins: Hold regular meetings to align goals and values.

Reflection Activity:

- How is your team in alignment with your vision and values?
- What are some things you can do to strengthen that alignment?

Lessons from the Butterfly: Harmony Enables Flight

A butterfly's wings have to move in perfect harmony to propel it forward. Likewise, your business systems and leadership work together harmoniously to reach sustainable levels of success. This balance allows you to lead with confidence and navigate challenges with resilience.

Reflection Activity:

- Write down one area where your leadership and business systems feel out of sync.
- Identify three actions to realign them this week.
- Track the effect of these changes over the next month.

Key Take Away: Harmony Fuels Growth. Success isn't just about having the best systems or the best mindset, it's about integrating the two. When you align operational excellence with inspired leadership, you create a thriving business while empowering yourself to grow as a leader. The synergy between leadership and systems forms the foundation for long-term growth and success.

Call to Action: Create Harmony
1. Select one process or system to improve this week.
2. Reflect on how your vision as a leader is reflected in what the business is doing.
3. Write down one adjustment that will increase the alignment and congruence within the business.

When you thrive with intention, success is no longer seasonal, it becomes sustainable. But sustainability is not the end of the journey. It's the moment you realize that what you've built is strong enough to hold not only your vision, but the growth of others. Harmony between business and leadership creates a foundation, but legacy is built when that foundation becomes a launchpad for someone else. In the next chapter, you'll step into a new dimension of leadership, one where you guide others into flight, multiply your impact, and lead from a place of alignment that expands beyond you.

CHAPTER 11

Leading Others into Flight: Multiplying Greatness Beyond Yourself

It's a quiet, often unexpected moment when you realize the breakthrough wasn't just for you.

You've done the deep work. You've restructured your business. You've reclaimed your voice. You've aligned your goals with your capacity and your calling.

You're soaring.

But as the wind beneath your wings steadies, you begin to notice something: there are others watching. Some are walking behind you. Some are standing still. Some peeking over the edge of their own cocoon, wondering what flight could look like for them.

And they need more than motivation.

They need someone who's done the work not perfectly, but intentionally. Someone who's built something real. Someone who can show them not just what to do but how to be.

That someone is you.

The True Nature of Flight

In nature, butterflies don't fly merely to escape the cocoon. Their emergence is not an end, it is a beginning. Once airborne, they become agents of growth, landing from flower to flower, transferring pollen, initiating new life, and sustaining the ecosystem they are part of.

Their flight is purposeful. It is generative.

The same is true in business and leadership.

You were never meant to be the only one who flourished.
Your growth was never meant to live in isolation.
You are here to activate something far greater than yourself, to create the kind of environment where others can rise and find their own wings.

That is the true nature of flight.

To lead others into flight is to do more than inspire. It is to design space, cultivate readiness, and build structures where others can thrive, not in your shadow, but in the light of what your leadership has made possible.

It means welcoming others into systems that aren't dependent on your control, but are strong enough to guide them toward their own becoming.
It means releasing the need to have every answer, and instead becoming a trusted guide who teaches others how to find their own.
It means multiplying not just revenue, not just outcomes but alignment, courage, and capacity.

This is the final act of transformation, when your leadership becomes legacy.

The Shift from Center to Catalyst

Earlier in your journey, the work was inward.
The questions centered around you:

- What do I need?
- What's holding me back?
- What does success look like for me?

This focus was necessary. You were breaking ground, redefining your identity, restructuring your business, and rewriting your relationship with leadership.

But now, the lens widens.

- Who else is ready to grow and needs a container to do so?
- Who is silently watching, waiting for permission to rise?
- What can I build that nurtures leadership in others?

This is where ego gives way to ecosystem. The turning point in leadership where the focus shifts from self-centered achievement (*ego*) to shared growth and sustainable impact (*ecosystem*).

Ego represents:

- Needing to do everything yourself.
- Holding onto control.
- Seeking validation or recognition.
- Operating from "I built this. I lead this. I need to be seen."

Ecosystem represents:

- Creating systems that empower others.
- Letting go of the need to be the only expert.
- Designing structures where others can thrive, even in your absence.

- Operating from "This lives beyond me. Others can grow within what I've built."

You are no longer proving your value.
You are positioning others to discover theirs.

Your presence now serves as a launchpad, not a spotlight.
Your systems, the very ones you struggled to build, now become blueprints for others to grow inside.
Your leadership becomes less about being at the center, and more about creating centers of growth all around you.

You are not just leading.
You are multiplying leadership.
And that is the highest expression of transformation.

Designing Leadership Pathways

Leadership replication isn't accidental.
It's intentional. Strategic. Rooted in the same G.R.E.A.T. alignment you've used to build your business and evolve as a leader. The same way you designed your foundation with clarity, structure, and soul, is how you now design environments where others can grow.

You don't just hand over tasks. You pass on belief.
You don't simply delegate, you develop.
Because greatness, when built right, becomes generative.

Let's walk through how the G.R.E.A.T. Ecosystem™ extends from you to those you lead, mentor, or nurture in your community.

Applying the G.R.E.A.T. Framework™ with Others

Goals: Start by sharing the vision, not just what you're building, but why it matters. When people connect to a mission larger than their task list, they show up with ownership, not obligation.

Review: Create regular rhythms for reflection, not just performance checks. Ask: What's working for you? What's feeling misaligned? When people feel heard, they engage more deeply and lead more authentically.

Evaluate: Invite them into the decision-making process. Don't hoard strategy, teach it. Help them think critically, understand context, and connect their role to the bigger picture.

Action: Give them space to lead. Let them take the reins on something real, not perform for you, but build something of their own inside your vision. Delegate authority, not just assignments.

Thrive: Celebrate not just outcomes, but evolution. Acknowledge their progress, their process, and their presence. Growth isn't just in the goals met, it's in the person rising.

Activating the Greatness Within Framework™ in Mentorship

Mentorship is not about creating a copy of yourself, it's about helping someone meet their own reflection and rise into their unique potential.

Groundwork: Ask them who they are becoming. Not just what they want to achieve, but what kind of leader they desire to be. This begins with identity, not output.

Resilience: Allow room for safe failure. Share your story not just in victories, but in moments of vulnerability and growth. Let them see that setbacks are part of the process not a sign of weakness, but a pathway to wisdom. Show them what bouncing back looks like with dignity, clarity, and grace.

Establish Trust: Lead with transparency. Say what's true. Let them see that strong leadership includes mistakes, questions, and growth edges. Trust is built when we drop the performance and show up real.

Action-Oriented Leadership: Model decisiveness. Let them witness how you move, how you navigate resistance, take bold steps, and recalibrate when needed. Action inspires action.

Thrive in Balance: Teach them the rhythm of sustainable success. Encourage rest, boundaries, and joy as non-negotiables. You're not just shaping professionals, you're nurturing whole, grounded leaders who know how to thrive beyond the work.

Setting G.R.E.A.T. Goals™ Together

When working with your team or mentees, don't impose goals, help them design their own using the G.R.E.A.T. Goals™ framework.

Grounded: Guide them to root their goals with purpose, not pressure. What matters most to them? What's aligned with their personal mission?

Reviewed: Create a cadence of revisiting their goals with intention. Not as a checklist, but as a compass. Invite honesty, even when things shift.

Evolving: Remind them that growth is not linear. Allow space for revision. When goals are allowed to breathe, they stay alive.

Actionable: Help them break big visions into doable, meaningful steps. This isn't about momentum for its own sake, it's about movement that matters.

Transformative: Ensure that every goal leads somewhere deeper that it shapes not only what they do but who they become.

When you extend the G.R.E.A.T. Ecosystem™ outward to your team, your mentees, your collaborators, you are no longer the sole carrier of the vision. You are the catalyst.

This is how businesses become movements.
How leaders become legacy.
And how greatness becomes a shared space, not just a personal destination.

Jasmine's Next Chapter

You remember Jasmine, the founder who once sat in overwhelm, unsure if her business could sustain her, let alone anyone else. The one who, step by step, rebuilt her systems, reclaimed her voice, and designed a business rooted in rhythm and purpose.

But Jasmine didn't stop at her own transformation.

Three months after relaunching her ritual subscription box, she hired her first part-time fulfillment assistant, a thoughtful, curious young woman named Aaliyah, who had dreams of launching her own product-based brand. At first, Jasmine hesitated. She wondered, *"Am I really ready to lead someone else?"* But she trusted her framework and the woman she had become.

She didn't just hand Aaliyah a task list. She shared her journey. She pulled back the curtain and offered access: her packaging process, her supplier list, her lessons from missteps. She created clear systems, documented her workflow, and trained her not just to follow instructions, but to understand why things worked the way they did.

Jasmine asked for feedback. She invited ownership. She built a rhythm that allowed Aaliyah to grow with confidence, not dependency.

By the end of the year, Aaliyah launched her own Etsy store and Jasmine wasn't threatened. She was proud. She had built more than a team. She had built a launchpad.

Jasmine didn't lose her assistant. She multiplied her impact, not through control, but through design.

This is what it means to lead others into flight.

Activity Reflection: Who Are You Pollinating?

Let this moment ground you in a new form of power.
- Who are you mentoring, formally or informally?
- Where can you release control to make room for someone else to rise?
- What part of your process could become a framework, a system, or a path for others to walk?

Great leaders don't just fly. They build wind beneath other people's wings.

The Garden You're Building

Your work matters, and so does your alignment. But the impact of your transformation becomes exponential the moment you stop holding it alone. You've done the work. You've tended the soil, emerged from the cocoon, and taken flight. Now, it's time to pollinate, to extend your growth into the lives, spaces, and systems around you. Let your garden become a movement. Let your leadership become a legacy. Let your greatness grow in every life you touch.

This is the full-circle moment of your journey where everything you've built now builds others. By extending the G.R.E.A.T. Ecosystem™ beyond yourself, your leadership shifts from self-driven to service-driven, from internal alignment to outward amplification. You are no longer leading for productivity alone; you are leading for legacy. The systems you refined, the clarity you reclaimed, the goals you aligned, they now serve as a pathway for others to rise. This is the design in motion. This is greatness multiplied. And this is the moment when transformation becomes contagious.

PART 4

The Flight Path:
Longevity, Leadership & Legacy

Sustaining Growth and Transformation

Transformation isn't a one-time event, it's a lifestyle. In this final stage, you'll learn how to sustain what you've built and embody the mindset and systems required to evolve with intention.

The life journey of the butterfly does not end when it takes flight. Every flap of its wings makes it explore new horizons, adapt to changing winds, and fulfill its purpose in nature's ecosystem. To leaders and entrepreneurs, transformation is not an event; it is a process. Growth must be nurtured, sustained, and continually aligned with your vision and values.

The Sustaining Growth and Transformation phase focuses on maintaining momentum in a shifting leadership and business landscape. It embeds the circular growth model into an approach to remind us that transformation is cyclical, not linear, with applicable actions for both maintaining success and continuing evolution.

The Circular Growth Model: A Continuous Process

Growth is not a straight line; it's a cycle. Just like the life cycle of a butterfly, the journey in leadership and entrepreneurship repeats itself. Each of these stages: foundation, introspection, implementation, paves the way for the next. To sustain growth, you must renew, reexamine, and realign with your purpose.

Visualize This: Imagine a spiral staircase. Each step represents a stage of growth, and as you ascend, you revisit familiar concepts but from a higher perspective. Sustaining growth isn't about starting over; it's about refining and building on the foundation you've already laid.

What Sustaining Growth Requires

Sustaining growth requires balance, consistency, and adaptability. It means evolving while preserving the systems and values that have led to your success. In this chapter, you will need to embrace three key principles:

1. Reflection: Regularly assess your vision, goals, and alignment with your core values.
2. Adaptability: Stay open to change and innovation, adjusting strategies when necessary.
3. Consistency: Build habits and systems that ensure steady progress even in the face of challenges.

Reflection Activity:

- How do you currently sustain growth in your leadership or business?
- In what areas would you like to improve your reflection, adaptability, or consistency?

What You'll Learn in This Phase

In this final phase, we will focus on integrating sustainability and transformation into your leadership and business practices. The following chapters will guide you through:

- **Chapter 12:** The Blueprint for Greatness – Learn how to embrace growth as a lifelong process by applying the cycle of reflection, alignment, and purposeful action.
- **Chapter 13:** Real Stories of Transformation – Discover how others have applied these principles in real-time and how your own story can inspire transformation in others.

Key Takeaway: Transformation is an ongoing journey, never really complete. Sustaining growth requires a continuous commitment to refinement, alignment, and innovation. By embracing the circular growth model, you ensure that your leadership and business remain dynamic, resilient, and impactful.

Call to Action: As you enter this chapter, take a moment to reflect on your journey so far. What has contributed to your growth? Which systems or habits need to evolve to sustain that progress? What small step can you take today to begin preparing for the next cycle of transformation?

CHAPTER 12

The Blueprint for Greatness: Embracing Continuous Growth

A butterfly's transformation does not end with its first flight. It continues to adapt, evolve, and explore, seeking new environments and challenges. Similarly, leaders and entrepreneurs know that growth is not a singular event or a fixed destination. It is a continuous cycle of reflection, learning, and reinvention, an ongoing process of striving for excellence while staying ahead.

The Blueprint for Greatness reinforces this idea, reminding us that transformation is a life-long journey. Leaders and businesses remain dynamic, resilient, and impactful by consistently revisiting foundational principles and cycling through reflection, alignment, and intentional action to sustain growth and success.

Growth is a Spiral, Not a Line

Many of us visualize growth as a linear path where each lesson builds upon the last. However, in reality, growth is more like a spiral, you revisit the same stages, reflection, alignment, and action, each time with greater insight and capacity. This cyclical nature of growth allows you to refine your leadership, adapt to new challenges, strengthen your business operations, enhance team involvement, and expand your impact over time.

Visualize This: Think back to a challenge you have faced, a difficult decision, a failed project, or a period of uncertainty. Now, reflect on how re-learning from that experience has helped you navigate similar challenges today. Growth isn't about avoiding those moments; it's about returning to them with greater wisdom and resilience.

Reflection Activity:
- What is one thing that you have revisited in your leadership or business?
- How has reflecting on that experience shaped how you now handle current challenges?

The Blueprint for Greatness embodies this continuous cycle, demonstrating the interdependence of personal and professional growth. You create a perpetual transformation loop through ongoing reflection, alignment, and intentional action, strengthening your leadership and your business with each cycle.

The Three Stages of the Cycle:
1. **Reflection:** Assess what's working, what's not, and why.
2. **Alignment:** Ensure your actions, goals, and systems align with your vision and values.
3. **Action:** Take intentional steps toward meaningful change and progress.

Each stage builds upon the next in an ever-evolving spiral of learning and improvement.

Mining Reflection for Insights

Reflection is the foundation of growth. It's the pause button that allows you to review your experiences, gain clarity, and extract valuable lessons. The goal isn't to dwell on mistakes but to learn from them and apply that knowledge to evolve.

Practical Exercise: The Reflection Journal

1. Set aside 10 minutes daily or a few times a week to jot down your thoughts:
   - What were your biggest wins?
   - What didn't go as planned?
   - What did you learn?
2. Then, review your journal entries once a month to identify patterns and track areas of growth.

Lessons from the Field: Real-Life Scenario

Lisa: Learning from a Misstep to Create a Successful Launch

Lisa had always been passionate about creating products that solved real problems for her customers. Her small business had built a loyal following, and she was eager to launch new products she had spent months developing. Confident in her vision, Lisa went all in on the launch campaign, believing it would be an instant success. But when the sales numbers came in, they fell far short of her expectations. The excitement she had felt quickly turned into disappointment, leaving her questioning what had gone wrong.

Instead of immediately scrambling for damage control or blaming external factors, Lisa took a step back to reflect. She revisited her campaign strategy, analyzed customer feedback, and examined market trends, determined to identify the gaps. Through the process, Lisa realized that while her product was strong, her campaign wasn't truly resonating with her target audience. She had focused too much on the product features and benefits rather than how those benefits impacted her customers' lives. The disconnect was clear: she hadn't effectively communicated how her product met their needs and desires.

Armed with this insight, Lisa approached her next launch from a fresh perspective. She engaged directly with her customers to better understand their challenges and preferences. Using this knowledge, she crafted a campaign highlighting her product's transformational benefits rather than its technical specifications. She incorporated stories and testimonials from satisfied customers to build trust and create an emotional connection with her audience. This time, every aspect of her campaign, from the visuals to the messaging, aligned with what truly mattered to her customers.

The results were remarkable. Lisa's next launch not only surpassed her sales projections but also deepened her connection with her audience. Customers thanked her for creating a product that genuinely met their needs, while word-of-mouth buzz attracted new followers to her brand. Looking back, Lisa realized that the lessons from the earlier failure had been instrumental to her later success.

Key Takeaway: Lisa's story highlights the power of reflection in leadership and business; by learning from past experiences and aligning your actions with your audience's needs, you can transform setbacks into opportunities for growth and create a lasting impact.

Reflection Activity:
- What is one recent experience from which you could gain new insights through reflection?

Realignment: Bridging the Gaps

Reflection brings misalignments to light, areas where your actions, systems, or strategies do not fully support your vision or values. Realignment is about addressing those gaps so that everything you do closes the gap toward your goals.

Practical Exercise: Alignment Audit
1. Identify an area of business or leadership that doesn't feel quite right.
2. Ask yourself:
   - Is this in alignment with my values?
   - Does it contribute to my long-term vision?
3. Create a plan to address the misalignment.

Example:
- Misalignment: Spending too much time on administrative tasks.
- Plan: Delegate tasks to a virtual assistant to free up time for strategic planning.

Reflection Activity:
- What aspects of your business or leadership feel out of step?
- What steps can you take to align them with your vision?

Act: Moving Forward with Purpose

The final step is action. This is where insights from reflection and adjustments made through realignment translate into tangible progress. Purposeful action ensures that growth isn't just theoretical, it becomes real.

Tips for Taking Purposeful Action:
1. Break Goals into Steps: Divide big goals into smaller, manageable tasks.
2. Establish Timelines: Set realistic deadlines to maintain momentum.

3. Celebrate Progress: Celebrate small wins to stay motivated.

Lessons from the Field: Real-Life Scenario

Raj: Transforming Workflow Through Reflection and Realignment

Up until this point, Raj had been an instinctive tech entrepreneur who prided himself on leading a team of talented innovators. The startup had grown steadily, with its projects gaining industry recognition. But as the workload increased, Raj began to notice the signs of strain. Deadlines were being missed, communication between departments was inconsistent, and frustration simmered beneath the surface. Productivity, once a strength of the team, was now faltering, and Raj knew something needed to change.

Rather than rushing to micro-manage, Raj took a step back to reflect. He set aside time to review his team's workflows and sought honest feedback through one-on-one meetings with his staff. What he discovered was eye-opening: the team was working hard but not efficiently. Tasks were often duplicated, priorities were unclear, and there was no centralized system to track progress. The problem wasn't a lack of effort, it was a lack of structure.

Armed with these insights, Raj proceeded to the phase of realignment. He mapped out the existing processes, pinpointing bottlenecks and inefficiencies that were slowing the team down. One major issue stood out: the absence of a unified system to track tasks and projects. Looking at this, Raj conducted research and subsequently launched a project management tool that his team could effectively use. This tool gave them a centralized platform to assign tasks, set deadlines, and monitor progress in real-time. To address this, he researched various solutions and ultimately implemented a project management tool that streamlined workflows and improved team coordination.

The changes did not happen overnight, but the results were profound. With new workflows and a project management system in place, the team quickly regained its footing. Tasks were completed on time, communication improved, and morale soared as team members felt empowered to take ownership of their work. An especially challenging and delayed project was finished ahead of schedule and exceeded client expectations by a wide margin.

Reflecting on the transformation, Raj realized that the real solution to the problem was the ability to pause, reflect, and genuinely listen to his team. By aligning processes with goals and providing the right tools for success.

Key Takeaway: Raj's story highlights the power of reflection, realignment, and purposeful action. By identifying inefficiencies and taking strategic steps to address them, leaders can create an environment where teams thrive and consistently exceed expectations.

Reflection Activity:
- What is one actionable step you can take today to move a goal forward?

Embracing the Power of Iteration

Growth is not a one-time event; but a continuous refinement, alignment, and expansion process. Each cycle of reflection, adjustment, and action deepens your insights, strengthens your strategies, and enhances your ability to lead with purpose. The most effective leaders and successful businesses are not those who chase perfection but those who commit to continuous learning and adaptation.

Iteration is the key to long-term sustainability and impact. It enables you to evolve, refine your approach, and respond confidently to challenges rather than resist. Every obstacle presents an opportunity to reassess, realign, and take more informed action, building resilience and expanding your capacity to lead at higher levels.

As you move forward, embrace the mindset that no decision is final, no setback is permanent, and no achievement marks the peak of your potential. Your leadership, business, and personal growth are dynamic and ever-evolving. Each version of you and every iteration of your business prepares you for the next stage of success.

The power of iteration ensures that every step forward, whether a triumph or a challenge fuels future growth. Stay committed to the process, trust your ability to adapt, and design your greatness with intention.

Reflection Activity:
- Think of one project or goal that you have achieved in the last year.
- Write down three lessons you learned from the process.
- Identify how you can apply those lessons to your current or future goals.

Lessons from the Butterfly: Growth Is Infinite

A butterfly's transformation does not end with its first flight; it continues to adapt, learn, and grow stronger with every cycle in life. Similarly, your growth as a leader and entrepreneur is limitless. Every success and every setback add depth to your journey, expanding your capacity and amplifying your impact.

Reflective Activity:
- How have you grown in the past year as a leader?
- What are areas you might revisit to further refine?

Key Takeaway: Growth is not a final achievement, it's a continuous, intentional learning, refining, and adapting process. Both leaders and businesses thrive when they embrace iteration as a strategy for long-term success. Sustainable growth occurs when you consistently reflect on experiences, realign strategies, and take purposeful action to strengthen your leadership and the systems that drive your business forward.

In business, stagnation is not an option. Markets evolve, industries shift, and customer needs change. The most successful entrepreneurs and leaders remain dynamic and resilient, viewing each challenge as an opportunity to refine their vision and operations. As you grow, so must your business, ensuring that your strategies, structures, and team development align with the next level of success.

The journey never truly ends, but with every cycle of growth, you and your business become more adaptable, scalable, and positioned for a more significant impact. Commit to growth as both a mindset and a business strategy; you will create success by design, not by chance.

Call to Action: Start Your Next Cycle
1. Take time this week to reflect on what's been difficult and what has been going well.

2. Identify one area in which you could more closely align your actions with your goals or values.
3. Take one intentional step forward today, no matter how small.

You've now practiced what it means to lead through reflection, alignment, and action. But growth isn't just what you do — it becomes who you are. In the next chapter, you'll see this in motion through the stories of leaders who have embraced their blueprint, lived the transformation, and led others by design.

CHAPTER 13

Real Stories of Transformation: Designing Greatness in Action

Transformation is not abstract; it is lived, experienced, and shaped by intentional action. Behind every success story is a journey of resilience, challenges overcome, lessons learned, and persistence rewarded. This chapter shares real-life stories of leaders and entrepreneurs who embraced intentional growth, using reflection, realignment, and action to redesign their paths and become greater versions of themselves and their businesses.

These stories prove that transformation is not reserved for the select few, it's attainable for anyone willing to commit to the process. Whether overcoming obstacles, pivoting strategies, or redefining success, those who approach growth with intention emerge stronger, more aligned, and better equipped to lead and thrive.

Each of these journeys serves as a testament that success is not found, it is designed.

The Power of Storytelling

Stories have the power to inspire, connect, and teach. They remind us that we are not alone in our struggles and that success often follows failure, change, and growth. Hearing how others have met challenges head-on and triumphed gives us insight, more courage, and confidence.

Reflection Activity:

- Think of a time when you had to face either a personal or professional challenge.
- How did overcoming that challenge shape who you are today?

Stories of Transformation

Story 1. James: From Micromanaging to Trust-Based Leadership

James ran a small, boutique marketing firm with a team of exceptionally talented individuals. His keen eye for detail and relentless pursuit of perfection had fueled his early success. But overtime, those same traits had become his biggest obstacle. James struggled to relinquish control, reviewing every project multiple times, rewriting emails, and frequently redoing his team's work. He convinced himself this was the price of quality, but in reality, his micromanaging caused bottlenecks, stifled creativity, and frustrated his employees. As a result, they began to disengage, doing only the bare minimum, after all, James would likely redo their work anyway. Meanwhile, James found himself drowning in a sea of endless tasks, struggling to meet deadlines, and losing sight of his role as a leader.

The tipping point came when the firm missed a critical deadline for an important client. Defeated, James finally acknowledged that something had to change. Taking a step back, he reflected on his leadership style and saw the pattern clearly: his lack of trust in his team was costing him productivity and their respect. Determined to improve, James committed to delegating more effectively and setting clear expectations. He worked hard to let go of his perfectionist tendencies and instead focused on coaching and empowering his team. Weekly check-ins became part of their workflow, fostering open dialogue, tracking progress, and celebrating achievements.

The transformation was remarkable. His team became proactive, producing high-quality work that no longer required constant oversight. Projects were completed more efficiently, and the office atmosphere shifted from frustration to collaboration. With the time James regained, he could concentrate on business development, securing two major clients that significantly elevated the firm's profile. Reflecting on his journey, James realized that great leadership is not about doing everything himself, it's about trusting and enabling others to succeed.

Key Takeaway: Letting go of control and empowering others unlocks potential, fosters creativity, and builds a thriving team.

Story 2. Sophia: Reinventing a Family Business

Sophia took over the family bakery with pride, eager to continue the tradition her parents had built over a few decades. However, it did not take long for her to realize that the business was struggling. Sales had been declining over the years as the bakery's offerings and branding felt outdated in an ever-evolving market. While loyal customers returned for nostalgia, younger generations passed by without a second glance. Sophia sincerely wanted to honor her parent's legacy but knew that without change, the bakery might not survive.

Her first step was reflecting on the bakery's strengths and rich history. She surveyed long-time customers to understand what they cherished most and analyzed industry trends to identify opportunities for growth. What she discovered was a way to modernize while preserving the heart of the business. She introduced new recipes, including gluten-free and vegan treats, to attract health-conscious customers while keeping her parents' classic recipes as a tribute to tradition. Sophia also rebranded the bakery, refreshing its logo, updating packaging, and redesigning the store layout to create a warm yet modern ambiance. Lastly, she built an online presence, launching an ordering system and leveraging social media to reach a wider audience.

The transformation revitalized the business. Sales soared as new customers discovered the bakery, while long-time patrons appreciated the seamless blend of innovation and tradition. Looking back, Sophia realized that transformation doesn't mean abandoning the past, it means evolving with purpose while staying true to one's values.

Key Takeaway: Change can breathe new life into a business and strengthen its identity while rooted in its core values.

Story 3. Daniel: Navigating Career Reinvention

Daniel had spent over a decade in corporate sales, steadily climbing the ranks and earning numerous accolades. Yet, after a series of restructurings placed him in a role he no longer enjoyed, he began to feel burned out and unfulfilled. For months, Daniel wrestled with this nagging sense that he needed a change, but he had no clear vision of what that looked like. The fear of starting over paralyzed him, so he remained in a job that drained him, unsure of how to take the next step.

One weekend, Daniel took time to reflect on his career journey. He listed every role he had ever held, highlighting the aspects he had enjoyed most. A clear pattern emerged, he had always found the most fulfillment in coaching and mentoring junior team members, guiding them through challenges, and helping them achieve their goals. This realization inspired Daniel to explore career coaching as a potential path. He enrolled in online courses to sharpen his skills, built a professional website, and offered free coaching sessions to gain experience and build confidence.

Within a year, Daniel successfully transitioned into a full-time career coach. His practice flourished as he helped others find clarity in their professional lives, and for the first time in years, he felt a renewed sense of purpose. Reflecting on his journey, Daniel realized that sometimes the path forward is hidden in the things you've already been doing—you just need to pay attention.

Key Takeaway: Reflecting on your strengths and passions can reveal a career that aligns with your purpose.

Story 4. Elena: From Overwhelm to Strategic Focus

Elena's e-commerce brand had grown rapidly, driven by her unique product designs and relentless determination. But with that growth came an overwhelming workload. Elena was juggling everything, product design, customer service, social media, and logistics. Late nights became routine as she struggled to keep up with orders, leaving no time for strategic expansion. Tired and overwhelmed, her business had hit a plateau despite her hard work.

One evening, Elena took a step back and mapped out how she was spending her time. She was shocked to realize how much of her day was consumed by tasks she could easily delegate. Determined to break free from the cycle, she hired a virtual assistant to handle administrative work and outsourced fulfillment to a logistics company. With these changes in place,

Elena was finally able to refocus her energies on product development and building strategic partnerships.

The impact was immediate. Elena doubled her revenue within six months and finally felt balanced and in control. Looking back, she realized that scaling a business requires scaling yourself, delegating tasks, and focusing only on what you can do.

Key Takeaway: Delegate strategically and focus on your strengths to create space for high-impact opportunities.

Story 5. Noah: Leading Through Crisis

Noah's event planning business had been thriving, with a packed calendar of in-person gatherings and a loyal client base. But, Noah's revenue vanished overnight when a global crisis forced events to be canceled worldwide. Facing mounting financial pressure, he knew he had to act fast to save his company.

Rather than giving up, Noah pivoted to virtual events. He invested in the right technology and trained his team to deliver seamless, high-quality online experiences. Now, he reached out to past clients, offering discounted rates to help them transition to virtual formats while assuring them his team would handle every detail. The shift was not easy, but his adaptability paid off. Within one year, the business rebounded. Virtual services, initially a survival strategy, became a permanent and profitable part of his offerings.

Looking back, Noah realized that adaptability is not just about weathering challenges, it's about positioning yourself for future success.

Key Takeaway: In times of crisis, innovation may turn challenges into opportunities.

The Common Threads of Transformation

Each of these stories illustrates a fundamental truth: greatness is not accidental, it is intentional. The leaders and entrepreneurs you've read about did not stumble upon success; they actively shaped their growth through a cycle of reflection, realignment, and purposeful action. Their journeys reveal shared patterns that highlight what it truly takes to evolve as a leader and build a thriving business.

For many, overcoming self-doubt was a defining moment. They learned to embrace discomfort, challenge limiting beliefs, and build confidence through action. Transformation required stepping beyond fear and leaning into the unknown, trusting that clarity would emerge through movement. Another key theme was adaptability. Rather than resisting obstacles, they viewed them as opportunities to innovate, pivot, and build resilience. Some redefined their businesses to stay relevant in shifting markets, while others reinvented themselves to align with their evolving goals and passions.

Perhaps the most profound takeaway is that success is not just about achievement, it is about alignment. Those who thrived didn't merely chase external milestones; they shaped their growth to reflect their values, ensuring that both their leadership and businesses remained fulfilling and sustainable.

Transformation is never passive, it demands courage, clarity, and commitment. Whether navigating uncertainty, rebuilding from failure, or scaling to new heights, those who succeed do so by design, not by default.

Reflection Activity:
- Which story resonates most with your own experiences?

- Where do you need to pause, realign, and take action to ensure your next steps lead you toward the vision you genuinely want?
- What lessons can you apply today to design your next level of success?
- What patterns of transformation are emerging in your life and business?

Inspiring Others Through Your Transformation

Your transformation has the power to inspire others. By sharing your experiences, lessons, and victories, you create a ripple effect, empowering those around you to embark on their own journeys of growth and change.

Practical Exercise: Writing Your Transformation Story
1. Identify one important obstacle you have faced.
2. Write up your journey using the reflection, realignment, and action framework.
3. Share your story with a peer or an audience that you trust for inspiration and connection.

Lessons from the Butterfly: The Flight of Shared Wisdom

The butterfly's journey doesn't end when it takes flight, it continues as it pollinates, nurtures ecosystems, and ensures life beyond itself. Its transformation was never just for survival. It was always about something greater.

Likewise, your growth is not meant to stop with you.

Your journey, the decisions you made, the missteps you learned from, the breakthroughs you earned holds wisdom. And when shared, that wisdom has the power to shift entire environments, just like a butterfly's wings influence the air around it.

Your story might be the spark that helps someone else see what's possible for them.

That is the flight of shared wisdom: when your transformation becomes a path for others to walk, a mirror for others to see themselves in, and a catalyst for someone else's next breakthrough.

Reflection Activity:
- Think of someone who has inspired your own growth.
- How did their story shift your perspective or open a door for you?
- Reach out and thank them for what they unknowingly (or knowingly) gave you.
- Then ask yourself - Who might be looking at your journey right now, waiting for permission to rise?

Key Takeaway: Transformation Inspires Transformation

Your evolution isn't isolated. It's part of a greater ripple, a rhythm that connects us through the universal truths of resilience, adaptability, and courage. The principles of the G.R.E.A.T. Ecosystem™ aren't just tools for growth; they are a blueprint for designing a life and business that empowers others. This is a living, breathing possibility, available to anyone bold enough to embrace it and humble enough to share it. When you lead by design, your transformation becomes a pathway for others to rise.

Call to Action: Write Your Story

Your transformation has power. It deserves to be seen, not just lived.

- Reflect on a challenge, personal or professional, that shaped who you've become.
- Use the Reflection → Realignment → Action framework to map the path you walked.
- Then share it with someone you trust, a team you lead, or a community you want to empower. Your story is a seed. It can grow something greater than you'll ever fully see.

This is how transformation multiplies.

These stories are not about perfection, they are about possibility. They reveal what becomes available when leaders choose alignment over autopilot, and transformation over stagnation. Whether navigating reinvention, reclaiming purpose, or rising through challenge, each person made the decision to grow by design. Now, it's your turn. You've seen what's possible. You've walked through the frameworks. You've reclaimed your voice, refined your systems, and realigned your vision.

So what will your blueprint for greatness look like?

CONCLUSION
Unleashing Greatness by Design

Your journey through this book has mirrored the profound transformation of the butterfly. Beginning with the Caterpillar Stage, where the groundwork for growth is laid; moving into the Cocoon Stage, a time of deep introspection, strategic refinement, and alignment; and finally, emerging into the Butterfly Stage, where transformation takes flight through purposeful action. Along the way, you have explored the delicate balance between personal evolution and business strategy, uncovering how reflection, realignment, and intentional action create a cycle of continuous transformation.

But transformation does not end here. This is not a conclusion, it is the beginning of your next chapter. Just as a butterfly's wings propel it toward new horizons, the tools, stories, and principles of Greatness by Design will continue to guide you on your journey of intentional growth and lasting success.

Reflecting on the Journey

Think back to where you started. You may have approached this book with questions like: Can I become the leader my business or team needs? Will my vision ever become reality? How do I balance my life, my work, and my aspirations without feeling overwhelmed? These are not signs of doubt or weakness, they are invitations to elevate your approach, refine your path, and design your success with intention.

In the Caterpillar Stage, you laid a strong foundation by identifying your values, defining your purpose, and setting strategic goals. You examined the core systems and structures needed to support sustainable success. Then came the Cocoon Stage, which challenged you to go deeper. It required patience and discipline, urging you to confront limiting beliefs, sharpen your decision-making, and refine your leadership style. Finally, the Butterfly Stage provided the clarity and tools to take action. You learned how to implement strategies effectively, build scalable systems, and lead with influence and confidence. But the greatest lesson of all is this: growth is not a straight path, it is a cycle. With each iteration, you return to familiar places but with new wisdom, deeper insight, and a greater ability to navigate the challenges and opportunities ahead.

Greatness by Design as a Way of Life

Greatness by Design is not just a framework - it is a philosophy. It is a way of thinking, leading, and living that fosters alignment, fulfillment, and impact. It reminds you that who you shape. what you achieve, and that the systems you build in your business reflect and refine the leader within.

When you embrace Greatness by Design, challenges no longer appear as barriers; they become opportunities for reinvention. Failures transform into stepping stones for greater clarity. Success is no longer defined by a single achievement but by the continuous learning, refining, and growing process.

Imagine standing at the edge of a vast horizon, with boundless opportunities stretching before you. The wings of your transformation carry you forward, not toward a single destination, but into an ever-expanding journey of growth, discovery, and leadership. On this path, ask yourself: What kind of leader do I want to be? What impact do I want to create within my business, my community, and the lives of those I influence?

Leadership is not about titles or authority, it is about influence, connection, and purpose. It is about lifting others as you climb and inspiring those around you to unlock their own potential. Your growth as a leader is inseparable from the success of your business because the culture you foster, the decisions you make, and the systems you create will shape your legacy.

Your Legacy is Designed, Not Discovered

Your legacy is not defined by the size of your business or the numbers in your bank account, it is measured by the lives you impact and the ripple effects of your actions. Every decision you make, every relationship you nurture, and every system you refine contributes to a legacy of resilience, adaptability, and growth—one that will inspire others long after you.

A well-designed business does not just thrive in the present, it endures. A well-designed leader does not just succeed, they empower. You are not simply building a company; you are creating a movement, one with the power to transform industries, communities, and individuals for generations to come.

Your journey does not end with you. Just as others have guided and inspired you, your story has the power to light the way for those navigating their own transformations. Your lessons, triumphs, and even struggles serve as beacons for those navigating their own transformations.

A butterfly's flight is not just about survival, it is about pollination, spreading life and growth wherever it goes. Likewise, your transformation has a ripple effect uplifting and empowering those around you. The more you embrace and embody Greatness by Design, the further its impact will reach, creating change in ways you may never fully see.

Final Words of Encouragement

Every obstacle you face is not a roadblock, it is an invitation to rise. Every misstep is not a failure, it is a moment of reflection, a pivot point redirecting you toward something more significant. Growth is not about avoiding challenges but using them as stepping stones to design the life, leadership, and business you were meant to build.

You already possess the strength, resilience, and vision required to create the success you dream of. This book has not given you something new, it has simply illuminated what has always been within you. Your ability to lead, your capacity to evolve, and your power to create is already yours. The difference between those who achieve extraordinary success and those who remain stuck is not luck, talent, or resources. It is intention. It is action. It is design.

When you fully embrace Greatness by Design, you stop leaving your growth to chance. You recognize that success is not found, it is built. You become the architect of your own transformation, aligning who you are with what you do and ensuring that every step forward is both purposeful and powerful.

But remember this: greatness is not about perfection, it is about persistence.

It is about showing up every single day, even when the path is unclear. It is about having the courage to lead even when you don't have all the answers, the curiosity to learn even when you feel out of your depth, and the commitment to grow even when progress feels slow. Because progress, no matter how small, always compounds. The choices you make today, the reflections, realignments, and actions you take, will determine the leader you become tomorrow.

So as you turn this final page, ask yourself:

- What will I do with the knowledge I've gained?
- How will I step into my power and create the life and business I envision?
- What does my next cycle of transformation look like?

The time to hesitate is over. The time to act is now.

You are not just meant to succeed, you are designed for greatness.

Go build it. Go live it. Go lead.

Closing Visualization: Soaring into Your Greatness

Close your eyes and picture yourself as the butterfly, no longer confined to the safety of the branch, no longer bound by the limitations of what once was. Your wings, vibrant and powerful, stretch wide, catching the currents of the wind beneath them. You take flight, not with hesitation, but with certainty, propelled by the momentum of every lesson learned, every challenge overcome, and every moment of growth that has led you to this very point.

Feel the air shift around you as you ascend. The wind is no longer an obstacle but an ally, guiding you toward the limitless expanse ahead. Below, the familiar terrain of your past - the doubts, setbacks, and fears that once held you captive - grows smaller and smaller, fading into the distance. Above you, the sky stretches infinitely, a canvas of possibility awaiting the brushstrokes of your next bold move.

You are no longer climbing, no longer struggling to reach, you are soaring. Every beat of your wings propels you higher, carrying you toward new opportunities, uncharted paths, and greater versions of yourself than you ever imagined. There is no ceiling here, no fixed destination, only endless horizons calling you forward.

You are limitless. You are designed for greatness. You are ready.

Now, Soar!

ACKNOWLEDGMENTS

This book is more than a collection of strategies and insights, it is a living reflection of the stories, lessons, and transformations that have shaped my own journey. It represents wisdom earned through experience, challenges faced and overcome, and the relentless pursuit of growth and clarity. Above all, it is a tribute to the remarkable leaders, entrepreneurs, and visionaries I've had the honor to walk beside.

To every business owner who allowed me into their dreams, thank you. The dreamers who stepped into uncertainty with courage, the leaders who rose stronger from setbacks, and the entrepreneurs who built with intention and resilience, you are the heartbeat of this book. Your breakthroughs, your trust, and your commitment to growth have not only inspired these pages but reminded me of the power of transformation by design.

I extend gratitude to my spiritual teacher, Ra Un Nefer Amen I, for instilling in me the discipline to hold the vision no matter how long it takes. Your teachings revealed the depth of my purpose and gave me the tools to serve others with clarity, intention, and integrity. You've taught me how to stand in divine order while walking this path.

To Edwina DeGrant, my editor, thank you for honoring my voice while refining it. You helped bring structure to my passion, creating a book that is both professional and deeply personal, clear and yet full of soul.

To my mentors, peers, and every supporter who has challenged, sharpened, and encouraged me, your presence has made this work possible.

And to you, the reader, whether you are just beginning your journey, reimagining your next chapter, or refining the empire you've already built, this book was created with your greatness in mind. May these words serve as a guide, a mirror, and a spark for your transformation.

Thank you for walking this path with me. Your story is still unfolding, and I'm honored to be a part of it.

With gratitude,
Rasheeda Frazier

www.ingramcontent.com/pod-product-compliance
Lightning Source LLC
Chambersburg PA
CBHW051622120626
46551CB00014B/1903